Brother Juniper's BREAD BOOK

7-12-94

To my Son Paul
an early Birthday gift
I love you Mom

2-14-94

Brother Juniper's BREAD BOOK

SLOW RISE AS METHOD AND METAPHOR

Br. PETER REINHART

Foreword by M. F. K. Fisher

Aris Books

Addison-Wesley Publishing Company

Reading, Massachusetts Menlo Park, California New York
Don Mills, Ontario Wokingham, England Amsterdam Bonn
Sydney Singapore Tokyo Madrid San Juan
Paris Seoul Milan Mexico City Taipei

Grateful acknowledgment is made to the following for permission to reprint copyrighted material:

The Scottish Academic Press Limited for permission to reprint "The Blessing of the Struan" from *Carmina Gadelica: Hymns and Incantations*, translated by Alexander Carmichael. Copyright 1990 by The Scottish Academic Press Limited. Reprinted by permission of The Scottish Academic Press Limited.

John Thorne for permission to reprint excerpts from his food letter *Simple Cooking* 25 (Summer/Autumn 1989). Copyright 1989 by John Thorne. Reprinted by permission of John Thorne.

Library of Congress Cataloging-in-Publication Data
Reinhart, Peter.
Brother Juniper's bread book: Slow-rise baking as method and metaphor / Peter Reinhart.
p. cm.
"Aris books."
ISBN 0-201-57076-9
ISBN 0-201-62467-2 (pbk.)
1. Bread. I. Brother Juniper's Bakery. II. Title.
TX769.R416 1991
641.8'15—dc20 91-6708
CIP

Sponsoring Editor: John Harris
Technical Reviewer: Gregory Kaplan
Cover Illustration by Jim Baldwin
Cover and Text Design by Ruth Kolbert
Set in 11-point Goudy Old Style by G&S Typesetters, Inc.

1 2 3 4 5 6 7 8 9—MW—96959493
First printing, July 1991
First paperback printing, October 1993

TO

my wife Susan,

who believed, who endured,

and

whose love sustained me.

Contents

PART TWO

APPLICATIONS

ACKNOWLEDGMENTS

I would like to thank the following people for their help, support, encouragement, and expertise, for without them this book would still be a half-baked idea: John Ash; Frances Bowles; M. F. K. Fisher; Peter and Robin Friedman; John Harris; Michele Anna Jordan; Greg Kaplan; Michael and Margaret O'Brien; my parents, Ted and Phyllis Reinhart; Susan Reinhart and Mischa; Charles Saunders; and Simone Wilson. I would also like to thank the staff, both past and present, at Brother Juniper's Bakery, and especially Brother Robert De Lucia, Karen Donaghy, Mara Jennings, and Sister Geraldine Richardson. I wish to pay special thanks to the Brothers and Sisters of Christ the Saviour Brotherhood and to the people of Forestville, California.

Foreword

BY M.F.K. FISHER

Brother Juniper's Bread Book could be written by no one but Brother Peter, and it is strange that it is not oppressively pious, as it would surely sound if he had not written it. I would say nothing about this book at all if I did not truly enjoy it. Yet, it is an odd book and, of course, Brother Peter is odd. One has only to read a sentence or two in any of his chapters to feel this strangeness, the peculiar sureness, and yet the almost shy part of him.

Of course, the best of Brother Peter's many good breads is the Struan, the legendary harvest bread of Scotland. Thanks to his and Sister Susan's never-flagging generosity, I've often eaten it, and I agree with every good word that has ever been said or written about it. I think I like it especially when it is a few days old and ready to be toasted. It also has a wonderful smell and makes exactly the right kind of "thunk," when it is . . . well, thunked. (Anyone who knows anything about real bread will understand this, just as he will agree that Struan is the best bread in this present world.)

Perhaps I am under Brother Peter's spell, but I doubt it very much, though he and Sister Susan are intrinsic to my life. Their own rather peculiar way of life seems quite natural to me, and I never think of them as being different from other humans. They are, though, just as the Struan bread is different from any other. And although I could give thanks daily for them and for the bread they make, it seems quite unnecessary. In fact it would embarrass us all. It is enough for me to be thankful that I know them and that I recognize this book is as much a part of them as the air we all breathe, or the words we all feel in our hearts, knowingly or not, about things that are true and simple: good air, good bread, good people.

Glen Ellen, CA
1991

PREFACE

IS THERE REALLY A NEED FOR ANOTHER BREAD BOOK? There are so many fine books already available, written by people with lifetimes of experience and creativity, that to add yet another title to the list may seem redundant and unfair to both the book buyer and the talented authors who have pretty well said everything there is to say about making bread. Therefore, rather than a book focused primarily on method and recipes, all of which, save a few original recipes that emerged from our small bakery in Forestville, are already available, I offer a book of commentaries that I hope will supplement and complement what most of you already know.

For those few who are, quite miraculously, discovering this as a very first bread book, there are enough rudiments to get you well started. Good fundamentals are—just as in sports, typing, and the martial arts—the key to success and the unlocking of creativity. This book may serve as a beginning in fundamentals for those who so need. But my hunch is that most readers may already be well-versed in breadmaking technique, though the fundamentals may need some brushing up, and are simply looking for something new or different. I know many people who are amazingly content if they can get one new recipe from their latest expensive cookbook. Having read a few myself I know the overwhelming feeling of seeing so many good recipes and knowing that I will never get around to making more than one or two of them. I have the same frustration in libraries and bookstores, wishing I could read even one-tenth of the books that seem to cry out for attention. Rather than add to this overwhelming backlog, I am ambitiously attempting to deepen instead of broadening the readers' breadmaking pursuits, not with any breakthrough techniques or technologies but, ironically, with old and recycled perspectives.

My analogical points will be immediately evident and probably cause the following response: "Yes, baking bread can be viewed as a metaphor for life but so can almost anything." To this I heartily agree and have received great joy and satisfaction from similar literary explorations in pottery, gardening, and motorcycle maintenance. The Bible, most notably in the New Testament parables of Jesus, has proven that the entire world, including the mystery of mysteries that is often called the "kingdom of heaven," can be explained through natural metaphors. What is needed, however, is for someone who is passionate about his or her metaphorical insights to take the time to spell them out. The hope is that you, the reader, will become sympathetically engaged in this same passion. The responsibility falls upon the author—me in this case—to direct your passion toward the higher, the nobler, the true, and the beautiful or bear the burden of misdirecting it toward the base, the dull, and the banal. With pen in hand I feel the weight of this responsibility and pray for your patience, and goodwill, and most of all, for good results. My goals are to leave you better prepared to understand and use the already available multitude of bread books and to deepen your passion and connect you or, more accurately, to reconnect you with the universal thread that allows bread baking to serve so well as a symbol for all that encompasses the meaning of life. If your subsequent encounters with either the process of baking or eating bread is somehow altered toward the good, the noble, and most importantly, the holy, then I will be able to rest more comfortably with the weight of my burden.

The Origins of Brother Juniper's Bakery

Many people have asked us how we came up with the name, Brother Juniper's Bakery, especially as we are not Franciscans. The original Brother Juniper was a monk who was part of Saint Francis of Assisi's original band. Stories about him in *The Little Flowers of St. Francis* portray him as a simpleton with a heart of gold who always manages to teach an important lesson about virtue to the other, more sophisticated, monks. The first Brother Juniper's Restaurant opened on Haight Street in San Francisco in 1968 and served a five-cent cup of coffee and inexpensive sandwiches to the street people and hippies. It was one of the earliest service works of our brotherhood, which was begun in 1968 under the name, Holy Order of MANS. In succeeding years Brother

Juniper's restaurants were opened in Boston, Atlanta, Indianapolis, Amsterdam (Holland), Portland, Oregon (where it is called Ezekiel's Wheel), and finally, in 1986, Forestville, California. By that time our entire order had entered the Eastern Orthodox Church and we changed our name to Christ the Saviour Brotherhood.

All the other Brother Juniper's restaurants were operated by members of our brotherhood primarily as breakfast and lunch restaurants and they all followed a similar format, serving creative sandwiches (such as The Happy Hermit, Abbot's Delight, and so on) and large portions at reasonable prices. My wife, Susan, and I opened the Forestville café as an experimental showcase for a number of ideas about food that we had developed. We planned to build our menu around original recipes we had developed with the expectation that some of them would be spun off into a separate, wholesale business. We thought that our barbecue sauce, affectionately called "Holy Smoke" (named by my mother), would be the mainstay along with a number of salad dressings and two natural herbal sodas. All of these items acquired strong local followings but nothing matched the intensity of interest generated by the breads, especially Struan. Every day, until we could not keep up with the demand, we would make a few extra loaves to sell. We rented a baking facility around the corner. A number of excellent restaurants began requesting the bread, and a local distributor from Petaluma, Tom Payne, began taking it around for us.

By this time Susan had herniated two discs in her back and had to leave the business for two years. Sister Geraldine Foster, Brother Allan Richardson, Brother Jacob Friedman, Brother Robert De Lucia and Father Stephen Steineck eventually joined in to keep the project afloat. We also had put together a crew of local Forestvillians, most notably Mara Jennings, who has been with us for our four years, and quite a number of students from El Molino High School. Little by little the bakery grew, the daily output increased, the variety of breads expanded. In the fall of 1990 we moved our baking facility from Forestville to downtown Santa Rosa, into a former *tortilla* factory. By this time we had already closed the restaurant and turned it into a bakery coffee shop. It was impossible for me to manage both a restaurant and a bakery and, with the bread sales taking off, it seemed clear that our future would be with the bakery. To this day people still approach me saying they miss our black bean chili or the clam and sausage gumbo, but circumstances forced our hand. We continue to sell our barbecue sauce at the café and one of these days expect to bottle it, and Susan's Greek salad dressing, Ginger Fizz, and other original products, for wider distribution.

It seems quite appropriate now that the bread became everybody's focus. Bread is really the perfect symbol for what we were trying to do with both the business and our ministry. As members of an Eastern Orthodox service order, the primary work of our life is ministry. With our livelihood coming from food service it is necessary to find a way to integrate our work with our ministry. A café offers a great opportunity for community involvement; feeding bodies is an analogue of feeding souls, and bread is the perfect symbol of the meeting of the two worlds. It is certainly a better symbol than barbecue sauce. I feel that God unfolded this business for us and we have merely responded with a great deal of effort.

Making bread in northern California, especially in Sonoma County, is risky business. There is so much good bread, especially French and sourdough, that it would be crazy to compete head-to-head with the already existing bakeries. We were fortunate, however, to have found a niche that no one else cornered. For instance, we seem to be the only ones who know about Struan bread (page 52). Not even the Scots make it anymore and no one knows what it really is supposed to taste or look like, so we were free to create our own version. This evolved over a four-year period during our Michaelmas celebrations, which is when I first began to make it. By the time we opened our café, I knew that Struan would be the wild card that no one expected and I hoped the public would respond enthusiastically. Soon people were regularly reserving loaves and telling their friends. Many people told me that they thought it was the best bread they had ever had. We added new breads and all have loyal followings, but Struan is still the mainstay of our bakery, and I still think it is the most beautiful and delicious bread I have ever made or tasted.

Struan gave us a direction for our breads, which are made according to traditional methods, in original formulations, yet are tied to folk cultures. The standard of our bread is that it must be so good that it elicits a response or a reaction when eaten. Neutrality is insufficient. We want people to be amazed by the bread and I would have thought this impossible with something as normal as bread but our experiences at food shows have proven that it can be done. We have, in fact, done it with each of our breads.

Impressing people is not a particularly great accomplishment in and of itself. It must be done in a context that makes it worth while or it is just an expression of talent or ego. The point of it all is the point of this book. I believe that spiritual discipline and practice, *ascecis* in Greek, is for the purpose of conquering the passions. Paradoxically, our business has been successful because it has caused people to become passionate about our product, bread. We encourage such passion and are encouraged ourselves by the passionate display we have witnessed. Christian *ascesis* challenges the human passions that bind us to our animality, called "the fallen nature" in theology. However, we have also witnessed a distinctly different, life-affirming passion that responds to things of quality and goodness. The ministry of our business has been to feed that hunger, to nourish it so that the energy of this passion for life can be used to do something positive. All we can do is stimulate it and give it a little nudge in a particular direction. We do not try to give it a denominational name. What we do is not so much religious work as it is a spiritual work, though it emerges from a religious orientation. If it is successful at all, it is not because our intentions are good but because our product is good. It is hard to get people to take your ideas seriously if you cannot back them up with results. We are fortunate to have been given the opportunity to create, in the context of an ancient tradition, a modern incarnation of a metaphor for goodness—bread worthy of its honorable name. It is this combination of factors that induces a passionate response which is, in my opinion, a very meaningful and therefore Godly direction in which to head.

PART ONE

GUIDING PRINCIPLES

Slow Rise: A Beginning

I LEARNED ABOUT SLOW RISE BY READING JULIA CHILD, who learned it from chefs, who learned it from bakers, who learned it from others before and before them. It is a principle, like a great cosmic law, that yields marvelous fruits when applied in conformity with other laws of baking and it is a principle that can, like all true principles, be transposed into the moral and ethical realms of politics, religion, work, and life in general. Slow rise is like saying "the Way," Tao, or *inshā'a Allāh.*

In breadmaking it works like this: You take flour, water, salt, and yeast, mix them together in the proper proportions, and form the dough into a ball. You then put it out of the way and forget about it for about an hour and a half. What you do not do is rush it by warming it up; just let it grow at its own slow pace. Then, when it has doubled in size, knock it down and form it into a ball again. Knocking it down causes it to develop character. If you bake it after one rise it will work but will not be very interesting. It needs more time. After another hour and a half the dough will once more double in size. Knock it down again. By now you have the makings of a very good bread, so form it into loaves and let it rise again for another hour, only do it right on the baking pan (so you can put it directly into the oven). Then you bake it. When it comes out of the oven, you have to wait because the bread is still cooking while it is cooling down. After another thirty or forty minutes, you can finally eat the bread.

Some slow-rise doughs take much longer than this, days even, but the point of the slow rise is that, when you mix the right things, you do not want to fool around with them too much. You want nature to work, character to develop. You do not want to rush the process. A world famous chili cook applied this principle to her specialty when she advised me not to stir a pot of chili too often while it is cooking. She called it "bothering the pot." With the right mix and enough patience, you can stretch out the process for an even more interesting character development. One of the keys is having faith in the process. Some would bake the dough after the first rise because of a fear that it will not rise again. It will.

While the dough is rising, life goes on, and other things are rising and falling too. One interesting fact about slow-rise bread is that the crust will be different depending upon how many rises you give the dough. We could conclude from this that crust is a definite aspect of character; we all love bread with lots of character.

Slow rise has taught me and is still teaching me a way to live, a way to be, and a way to see. It is a window into an understanding of the things that go on around me, a way to make sense of the seemingly senseless scenarios we are exposed to throughout life. Yes, slow rise is a metaphor but you might also say that it is a frame of reference, a context in which things find their proper place. You might also say, as I do, that it is the best way to make bread, bread with character.

The Sound of Crust

When I first began making slow-rise bread, I discovered a pleasure within the pleasure of the bread making. As a novice baker, I found every batch somewhat experimental; each loaf was an adventure toward some type of holy grail I romantically called *the perfect loaf.* My kitchen assistant and I would taste each bread before sending it out to the dining room where thirty or forty members of our brotherhood would happily devour every version. This led to a first corollary in my thinking: Freshly baked bread is always a hit no matter how it turns out. On one particular occasion, and I remember it as if it just occurred though it happened more than ten years ago, we took our customary sample bites and heard the crust crackle in what I now think of as the

Moment. I said to my assistant, "That's it! That's the sound! It's as important as the taste. It's the sound of perfection and it is so deeply satisfying!" Then I stopped my exclamations because my eyes were watering and I was beginning, in this perfect bread moment, to cry.

Coincidentally, around this same time there was a book, which everybody seemed to be reading, about the inner game of tennis in which the author identified a similar phenomenon about the sound of the ball when it hits the "sweet spot" of the racket. He discovered that, by learning to play for that sound, one's game could be dramatically improved. The sound of the sweet spot becomes, simultaneously, a striving, a beacon, and a satisfaction.

Though the "sound of crust" sounds similar to the Zen *koan,* "the sound of one hand clapping," there is also an important difference. The attainment of the sound of crust is like the culmination of a pilgrimage. That there is a sound that accompanies perfection is, in itself, a wonderful realization. It is comforting to know that beauty, which is a manifestation of the one universal perfection in its infinite guises, can break through into this world in the form of a sound that resonates with something inside of us. Such a sound is cathartic in that it lets escape, if even for a moment, the remembrance of the perfection that lies at the core of each of us. Beauty evokes beauty, love evokes love, and the sound of crust evokes an image of our being in the process of becoming. The sound of crust is what we hear when everything comes together in those brief and too infrequent moments of pure love, pure beauty, and pure stillness. The sound of crust, then, is not quite the same as the sound of one hand clapping because crust is an outer sound, entirely of this world, the outer world. Its connection with something inner is grace. The sound of crust is like an icon, not painted but baked, in which a window is briefly opened onto greater understanding. As beauty evokes beauty, the sound of crust evokes the intuition of perfection. When that intuition is sparked by something in this world, even crust, it can rightly be called religious, which literally means "connectedness." What I am saying, amazingly, is that the sound of crust can cause a religious experience, which is why I could not, that day ten years ago, continue speaking; why, when I heard it for the first time, I began to cry.

When speaking of crust with crackle we are referring to French and French-style breads. Crust protects the interior of the bread and it develops a character of its own that often becomes the most outstanding feature of a loaf. One of my earliest goals in baking was to make crust so good that kids would not eat around it and leave it on the plate. I now know how to do this.

Every book on bread will tell you that the secret to good French bread crust is steam in the oven. The common technique for this is either to leave a pan of water in the oven, thrusting a slab of hot metal in it during the bake to make a cloud of steam, or to spray the bread with a mist of water from a house-plant atomizer, a spray bottle (we call it a spritzer in our bakery). I prefer the spritzer. This technique is essential, but it is also important not to underestimate the quality of the dough, brought about by the number of slow rises it has undergone.

Anyone who has tasted the sourdough bread made in San Francisco knows about chewy, crusty bread. Sweet French crust tends to have a thinner, crisper texture. Sourdough generally undergoes a longer fermentation process, at least twenty-four hours, and the unique organisms in the sour culture cause the thicker crust.

Fermentation of the dough is the chief character builder in all breads. Each time the dough rises, more sugar is digested, creating carbon dioxide and alcohol. The trapped carbon dioxide stretches the dough, working, or developing, the gluten until a new creature is formed. Punching down the dough releases the trapped air, deflates the dough and enables it to rebuild itself to its former, heightened state. Now, however, it is rebuilding from a new level of quality—the dough is stronger, it contains less sugar and starch and more protein, and the flavors of fermentation are adding a distinctive character trait. The standard number of rises in French bread is three but I have great success with five. It is important to be sensitive to how many rises a dough can endure before it becomes alcoholic, which will cause it to taste yeasty and musty and weaken the gluten. (There is more on this possibility in the chapter, Too Many Rises, or the Pitfalls of Slow Rise, page 30.)

A baker is like an abbot, who serves as guide and guardian of the souls in his charge. Though there are general rules in a monastery that everyone follows (usually called the rule), each soul is unique and individual and requires a certain degree of personal attention. The name "abbot," incidentally, comes from the Aramaic word, *abba,* which means "Father" or, more literally, "Daddy." We are each, to the bread we are forming, as a daddy is to his child, an abbot to his monk, or an abbess to her nun, providing nurturing, discipline, and a clear definition of limits. Simply stated, the more nurturing a dough receives from start to finish, the better the bread. If the bread is nurtured properly with the right amount of discipline and structuring, a clearly recognizable and flavorful crackle in the crust will be the reward.

When the dough is ready to be baked, a few, well-placed slash marks are made with a razor blade or serrated knife. This controls the rising and prevents the crust from tearing as the bread bakes.

To get the crackle the oven must be hot—425°F. in a conventional oven and 375°F. in a convection oven. The heat sets the crust and quickly evaporates the surface moisture, crisping the crust. At the moment the dough is to be baked, whether there is a pan of water in the oven or not, spray the loaf with the spritzer. After two minutes of baking, open the door quickly and spray the bread again. Two minutes later, spray it again. Two minutes later give it one more good shot. This spray is the most exciting because a dramatic transformation usually occurs just before the oven is opened. The bread will have made a substantial oven spring, increasing in size by as much as 10 or 15 percent, rising to its fullness as the yeast cells complete their final feeding frenzy in the increasing oven warmth until the heat kills them, martyrs to their (and our) cause.

Approximately ten minutes after the fourth spray, the bread should turn a light golden color. When it does, give it a final spray and turn off the oven for a ten-minute, cool-down period. The bread continues to bake during this time, with much of the excess interior moisture evaporating. After this, the bread is removed from the oven but it is still drying out. The crust will be quite hard but it will soften somewhat as the moisture works its way out. Allow at least twenty but preferably forty-five minutes for the loaf to cool down completely. Your patience will be rewarded by a memorable event—the sound of crust and the taste that comes with it.

G·U·I·D·I·N·G · P·R·I·N·C·I·P·L·E·S

THE SOUND OF CRUST

- Nurture the dough through the slow-rise method, giving it at least three rises.
- Use a hot oven (425°F. conventional; 375°F. convection).
- Steam or spritz bread, especially during the first six minutes of baking, at two-minute intervals.
- Allow the bread to cool down for ten minutes in the oven and for between twenty and forty-five minutes after it has baked.

Sweet French Bread

MAKES TWO 1½-POUND FLUTES OR ROUNDS OR FOUR 12-OUNCE BAGUETTES

This recipe describes the basic procedure for making all free-form, French bread-style loaves, that is, for breads made with variations of these ingredients and not baked in pans.

At the bakery, we have to weigh our dough to insure that we do not sell short-weight loaves. Home bakers have no such impositions, but might find it useful to know that one loses about 2 to 3 ounces by weight in the baking: 27 ounces of dough will yield a 24-ounce (1½-pound) loaf. Smaller loaves lose less weight. This basic recipe produces 54 ounces of dough.

4½ cups high-gluten bread flour
4½ cups unbleached all-purpose flour
2 tablespoons salt, preferably sea salt
1½ tablespoons instant yeast or 2 tablespoons active dry yeast[1]
3 cups water
Polenta (see Glossary) for sprinkling on the pans

[1] Proof active dry yeast first in 4 tablespoons lukewarm water.

Mixing and Kneading

Mix all the ingredients except the polenta in a bowl (reserving a little water for adjustments) until the mixture can be formed into a ball. Sprinkle a little flour on the counter, turn out the dough, and knead it for about 10 to 12 minutes or until the dough is tacky but not sticky and has a nice elasticity.

Clean the bowl and return the dough to it. Cover with either a damp towel or plastic wrap, or put the bowl into a plastic bag. Leave the dough out at room temperature to rise for about 1½ hours. The dough will have doubled in size. Punch it down, form it into a ball, return it to the bowl, and allow it to rise again for 1 to 1½ hours. Punch it down again.

Forming Loaves

Cut the dough into 2 pieces if you are making flutes or rounds or 4 pieces if you are making baguettes.

To make flutes or baguettes, roll out each piece of dough into a long rectangle. Fold it in thirds, from top to bottom, and roll it out again, keeping the seam on the bottom. Fold the rectangle of dough in thirds again, crimping the seam with your fingers so that it will not open up. The goal is to create a firm surface tension that allows the bread to rise without spreading out sideways. If the dough becomes too tough to roll out, allow it to rest, covered, for about 3 to 5 minutes. This lets the gluten relax and then the dough should be more compliant. If it begins to dry out, spray it with water.

Sprinkle a baking pan or French-bread molds (curved metal cylinders) with polenta to prevent the dough from sticking and to give a nice crackle to the bottom of the loaf. Do not oil the pan as this will brown the bottom of the loaf prematurely. Place the baguette or flute, seam-side down, on the pan.

TO MAKE ROUNDS

If making rounds, roll out the dough into a long rectangle and fold it up in thirds as if making flutes. Before rolling it out again, turn the "parcel" of dough so that the folds are running vertically and the open ends are horizontal and parallel with your rolling pin. Roll out the dough again into a rectangle. Fold it up in thirds again, from top to bottom, and create a ball of dough by bending the parcel round so that the 2 open ends meet underneath and can be crimped together to make one seam. Hold the ball in your hand, smooth it out, and pinch the open ends together to seal them at the bottom. This bottom should sit on the baking pan on top of a good-sized sprinkling of polenta.

After forming the loaves, space them far enough apart to allow room for rising, and cover the pans with either a damp cloth or plastic wrap. Allow the loaves approximately 1 hour to rise at room temperature or, after 5 minutes, put them in the refrigerator to rise overnight.

BAKING

When you are ready to bake, slash the tops of the loaves either diagonally (3 slashes are usually sufficient) or, for the round loaves, in a tic-tac-toe or an asterisk pattern. A razor blade or serrated knife will work well.

Spray the loaves with cold water and place them in a preheated 425°F. oven (375°F. in a convection oven). After 2 minutes, quickly spray them again. Two minutes later, spray once more. Two minutes later, give another spray. You may want to rotate the pans 180 degrees after the final spray, if the oven is baking unevenly. About 10 minutes after the last spray look at the loaves. If they appear to be golden brown and done, turn off the oven and allow the loaves to cook in a cooling oven for 10 more minutes. Total cooking time is 26–30 minutes for baguettes and up to 40 minutes for larger loaves.

Cooking time varies according to both the size of the loaves and variations in ovens. Remove the bread from the oven, allow it to cool for between 20 and 45 minutes, and serve.

Baking Bricks or Tiles

You can approximate the effect of hearth baking by preheating baking bricks or tiles, sprinkling on polenta at the last second, and sliding the dough onto the bricks with a wooden oven peel or a long-nosed metal spatula. Bake as indicated, remembering the sprays. Round loaves, because of their increased bulk, will need 5 or 10 minutes longer to bake and to cool down than will baguettes.

When the Crackle Is Lost

If you want to restore the crackle to a crust that has lost it, which usually occurs a few hours after baking, spray the bread with cold water and put in a hot oven (400°F.) for 4 to 5 minutes. Eat the bread while it is hot but do not expect to use this trick on the same loaf twice.

Whole Wheat French Bread

MAKES TWO 1½-POUND FLUTES
OR ROUNDS OR FOUR
12-OUNCE BAGUETTES

This is made just like sweet French bread. The combination of one-third wheat to two-thirds white flour makes a light, crackly, and satisfying loaf. You can use any proportion of whole wheat to white flour according to your preference. More whole wheat usually means a slightly heavier bread that has a tighter gluten network but is perfectly satisfying. To increase the loaf size, allow slightly longer time for the final rising.

6 cups high-gluten bread flour
3 cups whole wheat flour
2 tablespoons salt, preferably sea salt
1½ tablespoons instant yeast or 2 tablespoons active dry yeast[1]
3 cups water
Polenta (see glossary) for sprinkling on the pans

To make, follow the directions given for Sweet French Bread on pages 10–12.

[1] Proof active dry yeast first in 4 tablespoons lukewarm water.

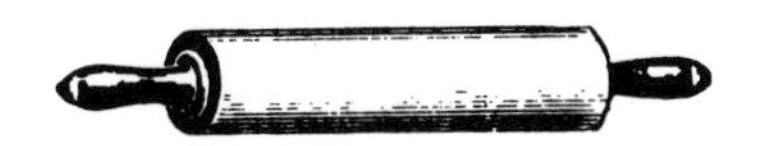

When Only White Bread Will Do

WHITE BREAD HAS TAKEN ITS FAIR SHARE OF knocks during the rage for whole grains. Most people who eat only whole-grain breads have developed a particular type of disdain, manifest in accompanying facial expressions, whenever they discuss white bread. It is not that the nutritively empty and tasteless "spit-wad" bread does not deserve scorn. The effort it took to launch a new awareness of the value of whole-grain breads was monumental. A complete reversal of attitude has been accomplished during the past two decades.

At one time in history white bread was too expensive for all but the very rich. The milling process was so complex that costs soared. Whole-grain (or brown) bread was for the masses, white bread for the elite. This caused an interesting caste system in which envy, a latent vice in all humans, created a greater demand for white bread within the working class.

Nowadays it is very chic to eschew white bread with statements such as, "I will no longer eat empty calories," or "All the good has been milled out," or "I never touch that flavorless, characterless balloon bread!" All those criticisms are true but it is ironic that white bread is now the staple of the masses and expensive whole-grain breads are the darlings of the rich and upwardly mobile.

There are, however, times when only white bread will do. I am referring not only to its importance for grilled cheese sandwiches or tuna fish or chicken salad on toast with potato chips on the side but, more significantly, to meals such as a beautiful supper of prime rib *au jus* with fresh garden vegetables, for which a perfect sop is needed. French bread will always do but there are times when a spectacular alternative is called for, one that makes a wonderful impression on the guests. Good white bread, baked in large bread pans and served on a cutting board, still warm from the oven, is so perfect for the occasion because it does not compete with but, rather, complements the juices and flavors of the entrée.

There are numerous variations of white bread, most of them made with sugar, oil, and milk. The recipe I use calls for none of these. In fact, it is simply a variation of French bread baked in a loaf pan. Once again, it is the principle of the slow rise that makes this the most exceptional white bread of them all. My theory is that the best bread is also the simplest: flour, salt, yeast, water, and time. The addition of anything else will change the texture, flavor, and crumb and will necessitate a change in time as well. Time is the ally of slow-rise bread and the enemy of fast-rise bread. It is also an adversary of milk and sugar additives because they serve as yeast foods, accelerating the pace of fermentation and thus diminishing the number of rises the dough can endure before it becomes overripe.

Because our palates and minds have been programmed to

G·U·I·D·I·N·G · P·R·I·N·C·I·P·L·E·S

FORMING ROLLS

- Two-, 3- or 4-ounce dinner rolls are easy to make and take less time than do loaves.
- Weigh out pieces of any type of dough.
- Cup your hand into a shallow hollow or concave shape and, on the table, roll the pieces of dough in a circular motion inside this cup, letting the weight of your hand and the friction of the table do all the work. The dough will round up nicely with a little dimple on the bottom.
- Pinch this dimple closed and set the roll on baking sheet that has been lightly greased or sprinkled with polenta.

  Two-ounce rolls generally take from 12 to 15 minutes to bake, 4-ounce rolls, 20 minutes. They should brown up lightly.
- A strong egg wash, 1 egg to 1 tablespoon water, will give them a bright sheen and will also hold seeds on top if desired as a garnish.

  Note: An unbaked, unrisen, 2-ounce roll is about the size of a Ping-Pong ball. A 3-ounce roll is the size of a golf ball. A 4-ounce roll is the size of a racquetball.

desire soft squeezability, commercial breads are filled with oxidizing agents such as potassium bromate, and dough conditioners, such as whey and cysteine (called "Reddi-Sponge," which should be a tip-off as to its role), skim milk powder, oils and other yeast foods. The result is a fast, soft loaf.

As an alternative, I am proposing a slow, firm loaf that will change your view of white bread forever. The nutritive arguments still stand and I would not make a habit of eating lots of white bread. But, when only white bread will do, we should at least make an event of it and it should be worthy of the foods it accompanies. Even a tuna or chicken salad sandwich, common though they be, are delectable and deserve to be served on slow-rise white bread whose flavor symbiotically enhances the filling.

I repeat: There are times when only white bread will do.

White Bread Loaf

MAKES TWO 1½-POUND LOAVES

This bread will not taste like other white bread. It will have an open gluten network, a nutty flavor, and a wonderful character. Allow it to cool completely before slicing for sandwiches or it will accordion on you. The ingredients for this bread are exactly the same as those for Sweet French Bread (page 9), the difference is that the dough is baked in pans.

4½ cups high-gluten flour
4½ cups unbleached all-purpose flour
2 tablespoons salt, preferably sea salt
1½ tablespoons instant yeast or 2 tablespoons active dry yeast[1]
3 cups water

[1] Proof active dry yeast first in 4 tablespoons lukewarm water.

Mixing

Combine all the ingredients in a bowl (reserving a little water for adjustments) until the mixture can be formed into a ball. Sprinkle a little flour on the counter, turn out the dough, and knead it for about 10 to 12 minutes or until the dough is tacky but not sticky and has a nice elasticity.

Proofing

Clean out the bowl and return the dough to it. Cover with either a damp towel or plastic wrap, or put the bowl into a plastic bag. Leave the dough out at room temperature to rise for about 1½ hours or until it has doubled in size. Punch it down, form it into a ball, return it to the bowl, and allow it to rise again for 1 to 1½ hours.

Forming Loaves

To form loaves to be baked in pans, it is not necessary to punch the dough down again after its second rise; the process of shaping the loaves will do that. Divide the dough into 2 pieces. (Each piece will weigh 27 ounces and, because 3 ounces will be lost in the baking, the finished loaves will weigh 24 ounces—1½ pounds—when baked.)

Flatten each piece of dough with the heels of both hands and then fold it over, back on itself, so that you are rolling the piece into a cylindrical shape. The seam that forms when the two edges meet when the dough is folded should be kept in one place, at the bottom. Squeeze the dough to release air bubbles and pinch the seam closed. Roll the loaf back and forth under your hands to smooth the surface. Place the dough, seam-side down, in a greased bread pan that measures 10 inches by 4½ inches by 3 inches tall. (You may use any pan close to these dimensions.)

Repeat the process of forming a loaf from the second piece of dough and cover the pans with either a damp cloth or plastic wrap. Allow the loaves approximately 1 hour to rise at room temperature or, after a 5-minute rise, put them in the refrigerator to rise overnight.

Baking

When the dough is cresting over the top of the pan, bake in a preheated 350°F. oven (300°F. if using convection) for approximately 45 minutes. Rotate the pans 180° about halfway through the bake. Test by thwacking the bottom of the loaf. The loaf should sound hollow and be lightly golden. Remove the loaves from the oven and allow between 20 and 45 minutes before cutting.

Time the loaf to be out of the oven 40 minutes before supper and serve it on a wooden cutting board with a knife so that the guests can cut their own slices. Have plenty of butter or margarine ready.

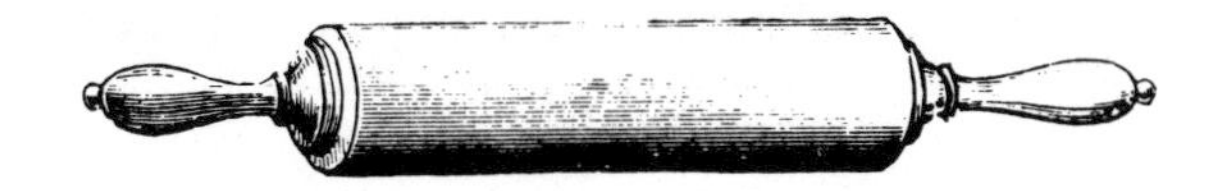

A Note on Yeast and Salt

THERE ARE DIFFERENT KINDS OF YEAST FOR BAKING and each works differently. Until recently it was considered cheating to use anything except pure, compressed cake yeast, which is the yeast residue collected at breweries, pressed into soaplike cakes, and recycled for bread production. It was thought that dry granulated yeast imparted an inferior flavor. But cake yeast is difficult to work with, cannot be stored indefinitely, is temperamental, and not always available.

With the perfecting of packaged dry yeasts, a resurgence in home baking began and, I believe, the belief in the superiority of cake yeast seems to have come to an end. There was a time, a generation or two back, when it was fashionable to eat bits of cake yeast. It was like a natural supplement and, I am sure, did no harm and may have done some good. Since then people have turned to brewer's yeast powders and vitamin B-complex supplements and bakers have turned more and more to granulated active dry yeast or, recently, instant dry yeast.

Yeast is not simply a thing. It is a fungus of which there are many strains, each with its own personality and flavor. Sourdough yeast, for instance, is a different strain from other bread yeasts, which accounts for its unique flavor. There are yeast spores existing all around us wherever we live, which is why sourdough can be made by simply leaving a sponge of flour and water out for a few days. One particular strain lives only in the San Francisco Bay Area and gives the sourdough bread from that region its distinctive taste. Bread yeast comes from the species of yeast called *Saccharomyces cerevisiae*, of which there are many strains.

Yeast companies have developed two types of dried yeasts. One of the most available is Fleischmann's Active Dry Yeast which, like other equally good brands, such as Red Star, must be rehydrated to be made active. This is done by adding a small amount of warm water, which wakes up the yeast. The whole point of doing this step, called proofing, is to give the yeast time to prove that it is still alive by releasing bubbles on the water. If bubbles do not appear, the yeast organisms have died.

Another, newer type of yeast is gaining in popularity. It is called instant yeast and I believe it is going to take over the market because it is easier to use and stronger, which means less is needed. This yeast is added directly to the dough, without need for proofing. We use it in most of our breads at Brother Juniper's and it is becoming more available to householders. Three brands that work well are SAF-Yeast, Fleischmann's Instant Yeast (different from their Active Dry Yeast), and Fermipan Instant Yeast. Most of our recipes are based on instant yeast. If you are using regular dry yeast, add 25 percent more yeast to the recipe and proof it before adding it to the dough. If you prefer fresh cake yeast, use three times the quantity given for instant yeast and proof it.

Yeast is leaven, which means, according to the dictionary,

something that changes or lightens a mass. It is used as a verb: "to permeate with a modifying or vivifying element." Yeast is like an alchemical agent that transforms base dough into pure gold (or at least a golden loaf). A little yeast raises the whole loaf and it does it in a sacrificial manner for, once its mission has been completed, it must die in order for the loaf to live. For this reason it would be honorable to respect yeast and to be aware of its propensities.

- Too much yeast can create a runaway loaf that will spring overly high in the oven. Too little yeast will run out of energy before it completes its work, leaving you with a small loaf or obliging you to wait so long to bake, in the hopes of continued rising, that the bread ends up tasting like yeasty beer.
- Yeast tends to work quickly in doughs that contain sugar, but it exhausts itself after two rises. This is why one rise in the bowl and one in the pan is appropriate. If you try to extract an extra rise from a dough that has exhausted itself, that bread, too, will taste like yeasty beer. When a dough (such as French bread) has no added sugars, the yeast works more slowly but can often sustain as many as three to five rises before the yeasty, alcohol flavor develops.
- If using cake or active dry yeast, be careful not to proof it in hot water, which will kill it, or cold water, which will not wake it up. The best range is between 100°F. and 110°F. It usually requires a temperature of at least 95°F. to become active.

Even though salt is just as important in good bread as yeast is, it suffers from an image problem. Ever since Lot's wife, Edith, was turned into a pillar of salt, it has had bad press. Though the Bible refers to humans as being the salt of the earth and, until the age of refrigeration, salt was the primary agent in food preservation, we try to be very cautious about using salt today. There is plenty of good reason to do so; medical evidence shows the frightening results of excess sodium, but salt is essential in bread and not just because of taste. It controls the yeast, moderating its growth, working cooperatively to bring about an even, slow rise. If we forget to put salt in the dough, it takes off faster than usual and the crust does not brown evenly. The bread tastes dull and flat. A little salt, like yeast, goes a long way. Struan is the lowest in salt (about one teaspoon per loaf) but that's because it has a fair amount of honey and brown sugar, which reduce the need for as much salt. In French-style bread (made of flour, water, salt, and yeast), the salt, of necessity, becomes the primary flavoring agent, worked upon by the fermentation process, necessitating a slightly higher amount.

Bread needs salt. If you have a salt problem or are on a restricted diet, try to eliminate it from other elements of your diet. The worst source of unnecessary salt is processed food. Stick with fresh. If you must, cut back a little salt in these bread recipes but do not expect the same results. Watch over the rising carefully and expect a bigger oven spring. Saltless bread is barely bread, though there are some worthy versions on the market shelves. I say this not as an insult but on the premise that what makes bread satisfying on so many levels is that its basic components are flour, yeast, water, and salt. With these ingredients alone one could make dozens of variations of bread. They form the staff of the staff of life; other ingredients are embellishments, points of interest, but not essential. Salt, like water, is an essential part of the staff of our existence; it is a component of ourselves.

Bread is more than foodstuff; it replicates us. It is not coincidence that it is used in the sacraments of all religions nor that simple bread speaks to us as does nothing else in the food kingdom. If you remove salt and yeast from bread, you remove the essence, the magic.

The Perfect Baking Moment

MOST PEOPLE TEND TO RUSH BREAD INTO THE OVEN too soon and end up with a small, characterless loaf. If you wait too long to bake, quite a number of other things can go wrong.

In one of the most delightful cookbooks I have ever read, *The Supper of the Lamb* (Pocket Books 1970), Robert Capon, the author, cautions bakers not to wait until the loaf is fully risen but to pop it in the oven while it is still on the rise. In a properly timed loaf, the oven spring, which can be as much as 15 percent of the total rise, will produce an evenly rounded rather than a mushroomed or flattened dome. If you wait until the loaf is exactly where you want it to finish and then bake it, loaf bread will mushroom and a French-style bread will spread out rather than up.

At our bakery, when we set up the loaves for baking the next day a similar dilemma confronts us. In order to be able to bake first thing in the morning, usually 5:00 A.M., we put the dough in the pans on the day before and proof it to about three-quarters of its final height. It is then put in a walk-in cooler set at 40°F., where at first it continues to rise. But, as the dough cools down, the yeast goes to sleep (which begins to happen below 50°F.). If timed properly, the dough stops rising just as it peaks and the following morning we can bake it off without further proofing. This process is called retarding and it adds an interesting dimension to the bread. When pan bread is baked cold, most of the oven spring is eliminated so it is the spring in the cooler that is important. When French bread is cooled overnight there is still a small oven spring (because of the spraying of water at two-minute intervals). In both cases, the overnight retarding allows a long final slow rise that improves both the flavor and the crust.

When loaves of bread are judged at competitions, one of the criteria is crust formation. Does the crust separate or pull apart from itself just under the dome? Do the stretch marks from the oven spring hold or split? Is the loaf evenly colored? Does the dome have a pleasing aesthetic quality or is it mushroomed, flattened, or split open? These qualities may not affect taste or flavor, but they are factors in the overall appreciation of the bread. Just as the sound of perfect crust can be profoundly satisfying, there is an aspect of visual perfection that is also undeniably nurturing when achieved. A perfectly formed loaf brings the same satisfaction to its baker as does a perfectly thrown pot to a potter.

Recently, I visited the Waterford crystal factory in Ireland where many of the glass pieces take over forty hours to produce and pass from one skilled specialist to another as they are manufactured. After the glass is blown into the general shape, it is inspected. If flawed, the glass is smashed and remelted. If not, it passes to the cutters, who carve intricate wedges and lines into the glass according to long-established patterns. Then each piece is inspected again and, if there are any flaws, the glass is smashed and sent back for remelting. Another cutter then develops more of the pattern and again the piece is inspected. The slightest imperfection and the piece is automatically smashed. At the final station, when the Waterford logo is engraved, the inspection process is repeated. Much to my chagrin as I vainly searched for an affordable piece at the factory gift shop, I realized that there are no factory seconds. There are only perfect pieces or smashed pieces.

G·U·I·D·I·N·G · P·R·I·N·C·I·P·L·E·S

THE PERFECT BAKING MOMENT

- Catch bread on the rise at between 85 and 90 percent of its final size. Expect the final spring to occur during the first ten to fifteen minutes of baking.
- If you are retarding the dough (chilling overnight—see glossary), do not expect an oven spring from your loaves unless you are baking French-style breads and are spritzing them. Retarded breads will spring slowly in the cooler, as much as 25 percent overnight.
- When retarding the rise, you may put the rolled-out dough, pan and all, inside a plastic bag or cover it with a damp towel or plastic wrap to prevent the crust from drying out.
- If the loaf falls, or loses the dome, before going in the oven, you may save it by putting it in a cold oven and then turning the oven on. While the oven and the dough are warming up, the yeast may revive and give forth one final push. If not, you will have to settle for a wrinkler or a flat-top.

We have turned out all sorts of loaves these past few years at Brother Juniper's. Some we sadly call flat-tops or wrinklers (see glossary). The really bad ones we just call losers. They almost always taste pretty good but they are not beautiful. We sell them as seconds because bread is much more forgiving (and affordable). I have smashed a few imperfect loaves and used the crumbs for a Country Crumb Bread (see below). But there is a limit. Fortunately, even flawed loaves are usually delicious and can often be consumed with great joy. Market tolerance does not always require total visual perfection and graciously allows for a small range of error.

But there are times when a loaf of Struan, the legendary bread from Scotland which is among the most beautiful breads I've ever seen has the power to stop production and gets passed around for all to see just for the sheer pleasure of beholding it as a piece of art. The catch phrase for such a loaf is, "That's a prizewinner." Every type of bread has its championship rendering. When all the preliminaries are done correctly and the moment of baking arrives, remember the oven spring (if the dough is fresh and not cold, usually 10 to 15 percent) or the retarding spring (about 20 percent, overnight). You will intuitively recognize the prizewinners and, if you can bear to cut into such beauty, will become delighted consumers of fine edible art.

Country Crumb Bread

MAKES TWO 1½-POUND LOAVES

For this loaf, save bread crumbs in a paper sack or make some from leftover heels and ends. Dry them out overnight or in a low oven, toasting them until the moisture is gone. Use a mixture of crumbs from different breads for a unique flavor.

8 cups high-gluten bread flour or unbleached all-purpose flour
2 cups dried bread crumbs collected from any kind of bread
2 tablespoons instant yeast or 2½ tablespoons active dry yeast[1]
2 tablespoons salt, preferably sea salt
Approximately 2¾–3 cups water (½ cup buttermilk may be substituted for some of the water if you want to make a softer, loaf-pan bread)
Polenta (see glossary) for sprinkling on the pans

To Mix and Knead

Mix all the dry ingredients including either yeast in a bowl, then add the water, reserving a little for adjustments during kneading. Turn the dough onto a floured surface and knead it for between 10 and 12 minutes. The dough will have a coarse look because of the crumbs but will be cohesive, stretchy, tacky but not sticky, and resilient. (In all of the recipes I use these words knowing that they will not mean anything to you until you actually make the dough. They will then take on a new meaning. In our bakery, the one catch-all word for a perfect dough is vibrant. But *vibrant* is such an abstract term that it cannot be used to describe what to look for in a dough. After making bread for a while, you will have your own mental equivalent of the idea of a vibrant dough.)

[1] Proof active dry yeast first in 4 tablespoons lukewarm water.

Proofing and Baking

Return the dough to a clean bowl and cover with a damp cloth or plastic wrap, or slip it into a plastic bag. Allow it to rise at room temperature for about 1½ hours. The dough will have doubled in size. Punch it down, form it into a ball, return it to the bowl, and allow it to rise again at room temperature for between 1 and 1½ hours. Punch it down again.

Cut the dough into pieces, 2 if you are making flutes or rounds (especially appropriate for this recipe; decorate the top with a tic-tac-toe design), 4 if you are making baguettes. Form and bake the loaves according to the directions for Sweet French Bread on pages 10-12.

The texture of the finished loaf will be coarser than that of other French breads and a little crumblier. It will be dark, like a rye or whole wheat bread, but it will have a distinctive flavor, derived from the particular blend of crumbs you put in it. This is what I think of as true peasant bread and it makes a terrific loaf for the picnic basket.

Too Many Rises or the Pitfalls of Slow Rise

WITH THE SLOW-RISE METHOD, WE STRESS MULTIPLE, long rises as a way to develop flavor and character. I have used this method for many types of breads but there are two caveats that need to be explained. The first is the possibility of too many rises; the second is that not all breads lend themselves to the method, Struan (see page 52) being the most notable example.

The best known bread in the world is classic French bread in its many variations. It is also the simplest in terms of ingredients but the most complex in terms of preparation. When you consider natural starters or sponges, levain-type slow-rise methods that take days, or hearth baking that requires high temperatures, the whole process can be rather intimidating. For this reason at Brother Juniper's we focus on the simplest methods and principles that still produce the highest caliber, prizewinning breads. There are wonderful breads being made by all sorts of intricate methods, many of them impractical for the home baker, except for the fanatical hobbyist. There are breads that only work if the grain is milled that day, if the temperature is constant at 80°F., if the starter is used only after it has been buried for a week in ash or sand to age, if made with a sponge method, if baked only in a certain type of brick oven, and on and on. Bread is incredible, even miraculous. It is almost always delicious, especially when just out of the oven. It is forgiving but only to a point. Awareness of some of the pitfalls of slow-rise breadmaking should allow the home baker to avoid failure or disappointment.

The multiple slow-rise method is specifically suited to breads made without milk, sugar, or other added sweeteners. It works best for the simplest doughs where nature is free to develop character in a simple medium. Complex breads with sugar, oils, eggs, and so on, added for flavor are best baked after only two rises, one in the bowl and one in the pan. For such breads, the character is being built into the dough by the baker (in the choice of ingredients) rather than from within by the yeast. Too many rises will cause an alcoholic dough and can, in some cases, develop so much lactic acid that the dough falls or splits apart while baking.

Simple French bread, made of flour, yeast, salt, and water, can sustain up to five rises but three are usual. The extra rises will affect the crust, texture, and flavor, usually giving a crustier, slightly more sour loaf. This may be to your liking so it is worth experimenting with three, four and five rises. More than that will yield a small gray loaf.

Struan, which is a very complex blend of ingredients, requires and demands only two rises. Any more than that and the dough changes dramatically. It develops a beerlike flavor, it splits on the top, it does not brown up properly, and it is no longer an exquisitely beautiful bread. This last reason alone should be enough to inspire responsible stewardship over the process but the other reasons certainly reinforce the necessity.

With some of the French-bread variations such as Cajun Three-Pepper or Oreganato, we have discovered that dough allowed only three rises produces a better loaf than does dough allowed any more. This is because the interaction of the yeast with the spices and acids impels the dough to slow down dramatically after the third rise. You are unlikely to get the dough to rise a fourth time but it is not impossible.

We discovered this by accident. The larger we made our batches, the earlier the Cajun bread-leavening qualities were diminishing. By the third rise it hardly had any vivifying spunk left. The primary variable in this bread is the spice blend, which includes a vinegar-based hot pepper sauce. One day we were out of our usual fast-acting instant yeast and had to switch to a different type, active dry yeast, which is slow and less powerful but steadier. The slower yeast did not seem to improve or even perceptibly affect the other doughs but had a dramatic effect on the Cajun. For some reason, the interaction with the spice blend did not weaken the leavening power by the third rise as it did when we used instant yeast; the yeast and spices were able to coexist longer. So, for this one bread, we use active dry yeast and have had great success. Since then we discovered an instant yeast, called SAF-Gold, specifically formulated for high-acid doughs, so we have two options for making this bread. Even with the slower yeast, though, three rises is the maximum for this bread. Anything more is a risk. At Brother Juniper's we now use the SAF-Gold because it is less expensive, but either yeast will work equally well at home.

I have tried letting a thrice-risen dough sit in a bowl overnight in the cooler and then attempted to roll it out and proof it the next day. Usually, the dough begins to smell yeasty and is very slow to proof, even when warmed. When baked, the loaf is usually thick-crusted and dense and does not color to a dark gold. This is another example of too many rises. The

G·U·I·D·I·N·G · P·R·I·N·C·I·P·L·E·S

PROOFING THE DOUGH

- Simple French breads (and variations): Use the slow-rise method: the dough, at room temperature, rises three times.
- Complex loaf-pan breads (doughs with sugar, dairy products, or other yeast foods): Allow the dough to rise twice, once in the bowl and once in the pan, both times in a warm place. Bake on the rise, allowing for a 10- to 15-percent oven spring.
- If using the overnight retarding method expect a 20-percent rise in the cooler overnight and a 5- to 10-percent oven spring in French breads. Do not expect any oven spring in loaf-pan breads.
- When is it done?

  Normally rolled out, unproofed dough will seem to fill less than half a pan but will rise to crest above the pan when it is ready to be baked—and then spring to make a nice dome, about an inch above the pan, when cooked.

dough has overfermented and the yeast is dying off in the alcoholic, acidic environment. If you want to make a dough one day and finish it the next, either put it into the cooler immediately for its first rise, punching it down when it cools, or give it two rises and then roll it out and place it in the pan for a final retarding rise overnight in the cooler. Retarding yields a superior bread with a beautiful crackly crust.

On Not Cutting into Bread Too Soon

SLOW-RISE BREAD IS A TEST OF OUR PATIENCE AND faith in certain processes. There is also a test awaiting at the end. The aroma of fresh-baked bread is an image that has certainly been evoked by authors throughout time and is an important element in the soul-satisfying qualities of breadmaking. Just as the sound of crust is an expression of beauty, the aroma of bread is deeply intoxicating and warrants its own poetics.

I heard on one of those National Public Radio programs that so often reveal interesting and little-known facts that the smell of bread in the oven is considered an antidote for depression. Something so primal that it cannot be fully explained occurs when one smells bread baking; it is soothing and affirmative and it chases the blues away. Having had many intense moments in our bakery fretting over mundanities such as accounts receivable, broken dough hooks, burned-out pilot lights, and whether I put the yeast in the dough, I believe that a good deal of what is left of my sanity is owed to the aromatic safety net that wafts through the atmosphere, supporting me in the midst of crises.

I have never been much helped by well-intentioned people who try to buoy me up when I am spiralling out of control with aphoristic niceties such as, "The Bible says: Take no thought for the cares of this world . . . consider the lilies of the field and the birds of the air. . . ." If, in my moments of despair, I could summon a consideration of the lilies, I would be glad to do so. The aroma of an oven full of bread, however, is the kind of strong unspoken sermon to which my nervous system can respond. The smell of hot bread is much like a lily of the field or a bird in flight, a message of goodness and divine earthiness.

The aroma of hot baked bread also carries with it a built-in pitfall for the unwary. Once the salivary glands have been engaged and the stomach juices triggered, it requires an act of utmost self-discipline to let the bread sit and cool. The mind is saying, "Hot bread, what a treat! The perfect time is now! Get out the butter!" But the will must know that the bread should not be cut for at least twenty minutes; forty-five minutes would be more appropriate.

There comes a time in life when a well-reared child has completed his or her education. The family has provided nurture, the system has fed and formed the mind, and a young citizen is on the verge of emerging. But there is a critical period during which the child and the parent are not necessarily in agreement about the timing of this emergence. The child, full of promise and vision, is ready to take on the world. The parent, weary and worldly, hates to see the young fire go prematurely into that ideal-crushing society. This is the bread-is-out-of-the-oven-but-not-yet-ready-to-eat stage of life. Haste has serious consequences.

The loaf, though out of the oven, is still cooking, "temper-

G·U·I·D·I·N·G · P·R·I·N·C·I·P·L·E

CUTTING INTO BREAD

- Do not cut into bread too soon! Allow the bread from twenty to forty-five minutes to cool down and complete its baking. Otherwise, the loaf will be doughy inside.

ing," and is too moist to be anything but doughy. The gluten is in the process of setting and the crust is deceptively crisp, hiding the immature bread within. If you try to slice hot bread, the loaf compresses, the weight of the knife crushing the unfinished dough. With the leaven killed by the oven, the loaf cannot just bounce back. It must complete its existence as failed potential, a could-have-been. I have seen many loaves, so golden and beautiful when taken from the pan, end ignominiously, with one large slice prematurely missing, the rest just sitting there, bypassed for other, more patiently treated loaves.

The intoxicating aroma of fresh baked bread can, indeed, chase away the blues. It can even make one a bit heady, a bit hungry, and, ironically, a bit anxious. If that smell can function as an active form of "consider the lilies . . . ," it is because it fulfills not simply a psychological need but a spiritual need as well. Transcending the senses through which it reaches us, it lifts our spirits toward the good, the hopeful, and the ideal. But, be warned, when you cut into bread too soon you crush that spirit.

Flour Is Not Just Flour

WHEN I FIRST BEGAN MAKING BREAD, I USED WHATever flour was on hand, usually unbleached all-purpose and whole wheat in some combination. After a while, somebody told me about high-gluten bread flour, which gives bread an added spring and lightness. Armed with only this rudimentary knowledge, we opened Brother Juniper's and began baking our own bread. One day a sales representative from General Mills dropped off a list of the different types of flour the company produces and I was surprised and intimidated by the variety. There are about six types of high-gluten flour, some made with hard spring wheat and some with hard winter wheat. Some are bleached and some unbleached. Some are bromated and some unbromated. (Potassium bromate is an oxidant that helps with oven spring but is considered potentially dangerous and has been removed from most brands as a result of complaints from consumers.) Some flours are milled for bagels and some for dinner rolls. There are as many varieties of all-purpose flour and again as many of pastry and cake flours.

What makes flours distinct from one another is hardness. Generally, the harder the wheat the better it is for bread; the softer wheats are better for pastries. Hardness refers to gluten and protein, which form the cell structure of the dough. When a dough is mixed, the liquid interacts with the protein in the flour and creates bonds that become the gluten network. Harder flours can absorb more liquid and usually require longer kneading to create the network. Softer flours, with less gluten, require less liquid to produce the bond, are unable to sustain long kneading, and the gluten network is weaker. Wonderful chemical explanations for all of this can be found, together with diagrams and photographs of gluten networks, in Harold McGee's book, *On Food and Cooking* (Charles Scribner's Sons 1984). When you see how and why some flours are tougher than others, it begins to make sense that so many different blends of flour are available. Home bakers usually have only three choices: bread flour, all-purpose flour, and cake or pastry flour, all of which are blends of a variety of wheat strains. Wheat blending is like grape blending in the wine industry. If a winery wants to establish a consistent flavor for its table wines from year to year, it blends a variety of grapes rather than depending on a specific variety such as Cabernet or Zinfandel, the quality and flavor of which can change dramatically each harvest. We have noticed subtle changes even in flour blends that are supposed to be constant because of the quality of a harvest or how long the grain has been in the silo. At the flour mills, chemists analyze the various properties of the flour and recreate as best they can the qualities that distinguish each particular blend. As a result, the home baker can usually rely on a general consistency within brands and types of flour.

What you really need to know is which type of flour works best in each bread. We discovered that French bread will be too hard if made entirely with high-gluten flour. The crust will be tough rather than crackly. A blend of half all-purpose (unbleached) and half bread flour yields a springy yet crackly bread. All-purpose flour alone will give an excellent loaf with less spring but a wonderful crust. Multigrain breads, such as Struan, are better when made entirely with high-gluten bread flour because the other grains have very little gluten of their own to contribute.

If you like the product of a local flour mill or have found a particular brand of flour at your natural foods market, start with that. Regular supermarket flour will also work. The quality of wheat and flour available in the United States is the finest in the world and the successful mills know they need to provide high-performance flours. As your breadmaking skills develop, you may find a flour that you are convinced is unparalleled. You may also be in a position to use the more expensive organically grown flours, many of which are of superior quality. But just because a flour is organically grown does not guarantee that it will perform better. More important is the type of wheat. Hard spring wheat is considered the best for most bread; hard winter wheat such as durum is especially good for pasta and for loaf bread. The soft wheats are reserved for cake flours or blended with a hard wheat to make all-purpose flour, which is excellent for muffins, cookies, and soft rolls. Cake or pastry flour is good for both cakes and pie crusts but will not hold the dome of loaf bread. If you want to soften high-gluten flour or all-purpose flour, you can substitute two tablespoons of cornstarch per cup for muffins, pie crusts, and cakes.

If you have a flour mill at home, you have the potential for the best bread of all. Remember, however, to pick and choose your wheat berries according to type. Experiment with blends. Simply grinding your own flour will not guarantee good bread if you have chosen the wrong type of wheat. When grinding, make only as much flour as you need. After the second day the flour becomes what is known as "green" and dough made with it is unsatisfactory. I do not understand the chemistry of this stage but, if you let the flour age or temper in a paper sack for about two weeks (during which it oxidizes naturally), it will yield better bread. Some mills, to save time, gas their flour to speed the aging, which is another good reason to mill your own.

There is a great deal of controversy over the merits of bleached and unbleached flour. Bleaching is merely cosmetic, designed to take out some of the natural yellow pigment in flour. It does not improve the flavor. Benzoyl peroxide is often used or, for cake flours, chlorine gas. Unless you desire the whitest possible loaf, unbleached flour is processed less and certainly white enough for white bread. Bread flour, however, is hard to

G·U·I·D·I·N·G · P·R·I·N·C·I·P·L·E·S

FLOUR

- **Bread flour** (also called high-gluten flour) comes from hard spring or winter wheat.
- **All-purpose flour** is a blend of hard and soft wheats.
- **Cake flour** or **pastry flour** made from soft spring or winter wheat is best for cakes, pastries, and pie shells.
- **Bleached flour** has been gassed to make it whiter; bleaching does not improve flour.
- **Whole wheat flour** retains its bran and germ.
- When milling your own wheat berries, specify hard wheat for bread, soft wheat for cakes and pastries.

find unbleached. Try your natural foods market and, if it does not have unbleached high-gluten flour, ask for hard spring wheat flour.

The amazing thing about breadmaking for most people is that the less you know about its chemistry and the more innocently and naively you approach the process, the more satisfying the results, unless you are prepared to commit yourself entirely to the hunt for perfect ingredients. I believe firmly in the integrity of ingredients and the virtue of seeking the highest quality. Conversely, though, a snobbery or elitism tends to poke its way into baking when people get to the point where only a particular brand of flour or only a certain yeast, cultivated, perhaps, on grape pomace, will do. Such limitations, when applied to breadmaking, are dangerous. There is an infinite number of ways to make a good loaf and the process is healthy whether or not your favorite ingredients are available. Do not be intimidated by baking esoterica of which there is an abundance. If bleached all-purpose flour is all you can get your hands on, make a loaf anyway. There is efficacy and grace in the process alone and the subtle differences come only with experience.

Buy Our Bread, We Knead the Dough

One of the most satisfying aspects of breadmaking is kneading dough. Much has been said and written about the therapeutic benefits of kneading, which range from the physical exercise to the emotional release, the psychological workout, and the personal satisfaction. In a bakery the bread is rarely kneaded by hand but by large mechanical mixers with bowls that move one way while a dough hook turns in the opposite direction. The therapeutic benefit is not a part of professional bread baking. Every step that a machine can do in place of hands makes the bread easier and cheaper to produce. At some point the bread becomes simply a product rather than a loaf, a commodity rather than a work of art or craft. If done correctly, however, the end result is still a delicious loaf of bread, as good as if hand-kneaded. So what is the big deal about kneading?

First of all, my interest in breadmaking was sparked because of kneading which was, from the start, the most enjoyable part of the entire process. The therapeutic benefits were undeniable, not merely theoretical. We have a cat named Mischa who takes great pleasure in climbing on top of me while I am in bed and kneads the comforter with her front paws. Staring off into space, she gets a blissed-out look on her face, but I can definitely relate to this mindless activity. The act of kneading dough can become a meditation if you perform it without distractions.

The most satisfying moment is when the gluten "comes out" and the ball of flour and liquid changes from a coarse, porridge-textured lump into a satiny, stretchy ball of bread dough. This usually occurs within ten to twelve minutes if the ingredients are correctly measured.

Kneading is an example of synergy, which theologically means the combination of personal effort with unearned grace. In breadmaking, the effort is self-evident, but the grace has to do with latent qualities in the grain and its potential to become something greater than the sum of its parts. This potential is a given, a gift, and has nothing to do with our own abilities or talents. It is held within the reality of wheat, yeast, salt, and water. The grace is self-contained but dormant until activated by effort, our effort, at which point the two energies come together and produce a beautiful ball of bread dough.

The dough has a discernibly different feel about it when this transformation occurs. It lightens in color, a slightly tacky but satinlike texture emerges, and all of the ingredients become integrated into an evenly proportioned wholeness. The gluten network becomes fully established, the fibers aligning themselves in the same direction and attaching themselves to one another, so that the dough can stretch and trap the air bubbles

G·U·I·D·I·N·G · P·R·I·N·C·I·P·L·E·S

KNEADING

- Make sure the counter is sturdy, will not slide all over the floor, and will not be harmed by the pressure of kneading.
- Work at different heights till you find one that is comfortable and does not strain the back muscles. You should be able to work from above the dough, pressing straight down, rather than across the dough.
- Leave out some of the water until the dough forms a ball, adding small amounts at a time, being careful not to create too sticky a dough.
- Flour sprinkled lightly on the counter helps keep the dough from sticking. This can be done each time you add water.

formed during fermentation. This is the primary goal of kneading; the therapy is a by-product or, in the spirit of the analogy, the grace.

Because the primary goal (the alignment of the gluten) can be accomplished by machinery, the biggest loss between production and home baking is the therapeutic aspect, the centering that occurs in the process of squeezing and forming dough. In our bakery we have to compensate for that in other ways, through our relationships with one another. At home, however, there is no need to relinquish this benefit.

If you possess a KitchenAid mixer or some other brand of

- If the dough is too sticky, add dry ingredients gradually by sprinkling them on the counter and kneading them in a little at a time.
- Use a mixing bowl and a strong spoon (metal or wood) to combine ingredients before turning the dough out onto the counter. Make sure the ingredients have bonded enough to form a ball. After turning out the dough, dip your hands in a little flour and begin kneading.
- Use the heels of the hands for most of the pressure. Press down, spreading the dough out, then fold the spread dough back toward the center. Turn the ball in quarter circles while you knead. Continue the process for ten to twelve minutes by which time you should either have a finished dough or know what further adjustments to make. If you find yourself adding more than one cup of extra flour, sprinkle in a few more grains of yeast and salt too.

dough maker, you are certainly free to use it without concern for the loss of quality. Mixers can accomplish the primary goal as efficiently as we can by hand. But, when you are working with small batches of dough (less than ten cups of dry ingredients), I would recommend hand kneading because, after all, there is no substitute for grace. If a batch of dough seems too large to work, divide it in half and knead each piece separately, combining the two at the end.

Try to schedule your dough making when there are not too many distractions so that you can knead in peace. Once the dough is formed and rising, you can resume your other activities but, if you establish kneading time as sacred time, you will enjoy the synergistic opportunity. Let the process of handling the raw dough ground you, connect you, and center you. But do not be pretentious about it; making bread is not the same thing as worshipping God or, as Van Morrison says, "sailing into the mystic." It is real, not surreal, which is why I enjoy it so much.

And Then There Was Struan

On the eve of the feast of Saint Michael the Archangel, a wonderful custom used to take place in western Scotland. Each family member baked breads called *Struan Micheil,* which were made of all the various grains harvested during the year. Usually the eldest daughter, under the watchful eye of her mother, baked the breads. Large Struans were made for the community and small ones for each family member. In remembrance of absent friends or those who had died, special Struans blessed at an early morning Mass were given to the poor in their names. Everyone then chanted an invocation to Saint Michael, the guardian of the harvest, and in praise to God for His ever-present blessing.

Brother Juniper's Struan is made from wheat, corn, oats, brown rice, and bran. It is moistened with buttermilk and sweetened with brown sugar and honey and, as far as I know, we are the only bakers still making a Struan. Susan and I went to Scotland and could find no sign of it. We went to the National Library in Edinburgh. Some research uncovered that it originated in the Hebrides, probably on the Isle of Skye (there is a placed there called Struanmoor). It worked its way to the outer island of Lewis where the Michaelmas tradition probably survived the longest. Struan dropped out of sight in the early part of this century.

It is a shame that nobody else makes it because it is an exquisitely beautiful bread. From our research, though, it seems that Struan was not always a light and pretty loaf. The original formula, according to the old hymn, "The Blessing of the Struan," seems to include a number of wild and crazy ingredients such as dandelion, smooth garlic, carle-doddies and cail peach, foxglove, and marigold. There was a stiff penalty if a young lass's loaf fell during baking: one year of bad luck. That could be pretty discouraging. Some sort of flour and egg batter was periodically splashed on the loaves while they baked to give them a thick glossy outer coating.

The greatest loss is of the ritual itself, the consecrating of such a concise symbol of harvest, of the diverse growth of a fertile land during an entire year, the loss of offering this symbol for a blessing, which is another symbol in the chain of symbols that ends only in the numinous. Struan is not merely bread—it is bread that represents the essence of bread, which is one of the great analogies of life itself.

In our everyday consumption of bread we tend to forget or lose sight of the reality of what bread is. So a bread ritual, a harvest fair, dedicated to the archangel of the harvest whose name means "like unto God," is a way to tune into this deeper reality. I believe that if the world falls apart, as it sometimes shows sign of doing, it will be as much because of the abandonment of festival rituals such as Struan at Michaelmas as because of war or pollution. Celebration is a lost art, a spiritual practice whose original purpose is sacramental in quality. That is why bread plays such a central role in festivals.

Struan is a harvest bread. All bread is, when you think about it, harvest bread. What else could it be? But Struan affirms the reality of harvest. Here's my fantasy about the ideal loaf of bread: I gather the wheat, corn, rice, and oats from local fields, then grind them myself in a stone mill, make a dough by adding milk just taken from the resident cow or ewe, and sweeten it with honey just extracted from one of the many beehives that we keep to pollinate the fields. Then I bake the bread in a brick oven fired by local hardwood and bring the still-hot loaf to the local holy elder for a blessing. After that I share the loaf with friends, strangers, and the poor. This is bread, the consolidation of all that is harvestable and all that is good about life on this earth.

Struan, because of its direct descent from a traditional ritualistic practice, still retains a trace of sacramental efficacy. That would be irrelevant, of course, if it were not also delicious. Perhaps the original Struan, with all its wild harvestables, was not as wonderful to taste as it is to ponder. But Struan, as it exists in its modern incarnation, resurrected, from a tradition that has died, as if it were a kernel of wheat dropped into the earth, is now a most beautiful, delicious, and wonderful loaf of bread.

A few years ago, when we had only just begun making Struan, one of our regular customers came into the bakery and told me that he was the son of a baker and had grown up working for his dad in their family bakery. "I know bread and I know what bread can mean to people. The children of Forestville are going to grow up and remember that Struan was part of their childhood and it's going to mean something to them. You'll see." That was the kind of testimony of which dreams are made. Yet it really happened and I deeply appreciate his articulation of my greatest ambition as a baker.

I have never given out the recipe for Struan before now because I believed it was important to steward something this special. I hope that, in sharing a bit of the history and meaning of Struan, you might also enjoy the blessing of Saint Michael the Archangel, protector of the harvest and of children everywhere.

Before forming and baking a loaf of Struan, take a close look at the dough. Notice the different ingredients held in suspension by the soft glutenous dough. Most especially, notice the little pieces of polenta floating in the dough, like little gold nuggets. Stretch the dough in your hands, hold it up to the light, smell it, and experience it tactilely. Enjoy Struan before it is baked for its many-layered beauty.

While it is baking, pay attention to the aroma in your kitchen. Inhale it deeply. Think about the fields where these scents originated and enjoy Struan for its "nose and bouquet."

When it has emerged from the oven, watch it for a few moments as it cools, radiating heat and moisture as it completes its bake on the cooling rack. The golden glow of this golden loaf, highlighted by the black specks of the poppy seeds, has an artistry that all breads approach but few, if any, exceed. Enjoy Struan at this stage for its simple visual beauty.

When it has cooled enough to slice, look closely at the texture. Notice the gluten network holding the golden polenta nuggets and pieces of brown rice and flecks of bran. The oats have almost completely disappeared into the bread. Smell the inside of the loaf, the hint of honey, the indescribable blues-chasing aroma of fresh bread, the slightly nutlike scent of the grains. Enjoy Struan as a completed bread, its components coming together to form the classic synergy—a whole greater than the sum of its parts.

Enjoy the taste of Struan. First try it fresh and without butter. Notice its flavor, almost like that of cake. Notice how the poppy seeds complement the flavor, not just garnish the loaf. See how the sweetness permeates but does not hide the flavor of the grains. Then try a slice with butter or margarine and see how it changes.

Finally, toast a thick piece and lightly butter it. This is the ultimate experience of Struan. All of the flavors are released, pushed to their extreme. The outside is crunchy, nutty, and deeply golden. The inside is soft and moist, soaking up the butter.

For all of these reasons, enjoy the Struan.

The Blessing of the Struan

Each meal beneath my roof,
They will all be mixed together,
In the name of God the Son,
Who gave them growth.

Milk, and eggs, and butter,
The good produce of our own flock,
There shall be no dearth in our land,
Nor in our dwelling.

In the name of Michael of my love,
Who bequeathed to us the power,
With the blessing of the Lamb,
And of His Mother.

Humble us at thy footstool,
Be thine own sanctuary around us,
Ward from us specter, sprite, oppression,
And preserve us.

Consecrate the produce of our land,
Bestow prosperity and peace,
In the name of Father the King,
And of the three beloved apostles.

Dandelion, smooth garlic,
Foxglove, woad, and butterwort,
The three carle-doddies,
And marigold.

Gray 'cailpeach' plucked,
The seven-pronged seven times,
The mountain yew, ruddy heath,
And madder.

I will put water on them all,
In precious name of the Son of God,
In name of Mary the generous,
And of Patrick.

When we shall sit down
To take our food,
I will sprinkle in the name of God
On the children.

Alexander Carmichael, *Carmina Gadelica: Hymns and Incantations*

Struan

MAKES THREE 1½-POUND LOAVES

7 cups high-gluten bread flour
½ cup uncooked polenta (see glossary)
½ cup rolled oats
½ cup brown sugar
⅓ cup wheat bran
4 teaspoons salt, preferably sea salt
2 tablespoons plus 1 teaspoon instant yeast or 3 tablespoons active dry yeast[1]
½ cup cooked brown rice
¼ cup honey
¾ cup buttermilk
Approximately 1½ cups water (the amount of water varies according to the moistness of the rice and the accuracy of the measurements of the dry ingredients)
3 tablespoons poppy seeds, for decoration

Mixing

In a bowl mix all of the dry ingredients, including the salt and yeast. Add the cooked brown rice, honey, and buttermilk and mix. Then add 1 cup of the water, reserving about ½ cup for adjustments during kneading. With your hands squeeze the ingredients together until they make a ball. Sprinkle some flour on the counter and turn the ball out of the bowl and begin kneading. Add small quantities of water as needed.

[1] Proof active dry yeast first in 4 tablespoons lukewarm water.

KNEADING

Because Struan has so many whole grains, it takes longer to knead than most breads, usually 12 to 15 minutes. The dough will change before your eyes, lightening in color, becoming gradually more elastic and evenly grained. The finished dough should be tacky but not sticky, lightly golden, stretchy and elastic rather than porridgelike. When you push the heels of your hands into the dough, it should give way but not necessarily tear. If it flakes or crumbles, add a little more water.

PROOFING

Wash out the mixing bowl and dry it thoroughly. Put in the dough and cover with a damp towel or plastic wrap or place the bowl inside a plastic bag. Allow the dough to rise in a warm place for about 1 hour, until it has roughly doubled in size.

FORMING LOAVES

This recipe makes about 5 pounds of dough (81 ounces, to be exact); to make 3 loaves of 1½ pounds each, cut the dough into 3 pieces—each will weigh 27 ounces. Roll up each piece into a loaf by pressing on the center with the heels of the hands and rolling the dough back over itself until a seam is formed. Tuck all the pieces of dough or end flaps into the seam, keeping only one seam in the dough. Pinch off the seam, sealing it as best you can and put the loaf, seam-side down, in greased bread pan that measures 9 inches by 4½ inches by 3 inches. (For detailed directions on forming pan loaves, see page 18.) Brush an egg wash solution (1 egg beaten into 4 cups water) on the top of each loaf and sprinkle poppy seeds on top.

G·U·I·D·I·N·G · P·R·I·N·C·I·P·L·E·S

USING THE OVEN

- Remember the oven spring. Do not put loaves on a shelf where they could rise into the ceiling, nor too low near the flame or coil where the bottoms could get burned.
- If the heat in your oven is not even (in most it is not), it will be necessary to rotate the loaves halfway through. If you are baking more loaves than will fit on one shelf, rotate the pans from shelf to shelf and give them a half-turn so that each side of the loaf gets equal heat.

Baking

Cover and allow the dough to rise till it crests over the top of the pan. Bake in a 350°F. oven (300°F. if yours is a convection oven) for approximately 45 minutes. The loaf should dome nicely and be a dark gold. The sides and bottom should be a uniform medium gold and there should be an audible, hollow thwack when you tap the bottom of the loaf.

If the bread comes out of the pan dark on top but too light or soft on the sides or bottom, take the loaf out of the pan, return it to the oven, and finish baking until it is thwackable. Bear in mind that the bread will cook much faster once it is removed from the pan, so keep a close eye on it.

Allow the bread to cool thoroughly for at least 40 minutes before slicing it.

PART TWO

APPLICATIONS

The American Passion

THERE IS ONE BREAD THAT RIVALS STRUAN AS A supreme toasting bread. We call it Roasted Three-Seed Bread and it is very simple to make, simpler than Struan, with a flavor that explores more deeply one aspect of Struan's appeal: the roasted nutty flavor that is so popular in our culture. Euell Gibbons once claimed on my living room television that some breakfast cereal tasted like hickory nuts. A few years later I had my first sip of Fra Angelica liqueur, which is made from roasted hazelnuts. Since then, the idea and the taste of roasted nuts have fascinated me. My fingers still bear the scars and stains of red pistachios from childhood, peanuts are a national passion, and pecans and macadamias are nirvana inducing. Being a product of this society I can only conclude that I speak for many when declaring these truths as self-evident, that roasted nuts strike chords almost as deep as those of fresh bread.

When we tested our first batch of Roasted Three-Seed Bread, the response was overwhelming. We were among thirty food producers, many of gourmet products, offering free tastes of our bread amidst others offering tastes of fresh oysters, *pâtés* with truffles, fancy cakes, pastries and croissants, pasta with wild mushrooms, and so on. I used to be intimidated at these events until experience revealed that good bread is more appealing than fancy food, once the first rush for the epicurean goodies passes. Again and again people returned to our table for just one more bite of bread, any bread, while comparing notes on the fancier foods.

The day we introduced Roasted Three-Seed Bread we were unprepared for the reaction. Passion, raw passion, came at us in the form of statements such as "God, isn't that to die for!" or "What do you mean it's not available at the markets! When will it be available? When!" I attribute this reaction to the combination of two passion-inducing flavors compounding each other in one product, those of bread and roasted nuts or seeds. This combination is hinted at in Struan, with its multigrains and poppy seeds. But, while Struan hints at it, Roasted Three-Seed Bread powers its way down that avenue like a fullback breaking off tackle near the goal line. Struan radiates in many directions; Roasted Three-Seed goes madly for broke.

Our formula for this bread does not use nuts, though you can substitute them for the seeds if you would like to experiment. I chose sunflower, pumpkin, and flax seeds because they are good for you, toast well, taste great, and complement one another. Flax is good for the digestion, pumpkin has lots of zinc, which is especially good for the prostate gland, and sunflower is high in protein and calcium. The key to maximum flavor is roasting the seeds first, which brings out the nutty flavors, but they can also be added unroasted to the dough. In most of our breads we like to make sure that there is plenty of fiber, so the recipe calls for the addition of bran.

Roasted Three-Seed Bread makes superior toast because then the roasted flavors are accentuated. Just as Struan is a bread that expresses the western soul, I believe Roasted Three-Seed is an expression of the distinctively American soul with its emphasis on extremes and epitomes. This bread is the epitome of a certain tendency, a specific kind of passion, that is very American. I think you will see what I mean only after tasting this bread.

Roasted Three-Seed Bread

MAKES TWO 2-POUND LOAVES

Wonderfully aromatic, this bread has a pleasant nutlike flavor. Sweetened only by honey, the soft texture is created by the addition of fresh buttermilk. Roasted pumpkin, sunflower, and flax seeds are combined with wheat bran and flour to form a bread suited to all kinds of soups, sandwiches, *pâtés*, and hors d'oeuvres.

½ cup pumpkin seeds
½ cup sunflower seeds
1 tablespoon flax seeds
8 cups high-gluten bread flour or unbleached all-purpose flour
½ cup wheat bran

2 tablespoons instant yeast or 2½ tablespoons active dry yeast[1]
2 tablespoons salt, preferably sea salt
½ cup honey
½ cup buttermilk
Approximately 1¾–2 cups water

Mix the seeds together and roast or toast them in a frying pan or in the oven till they start crackling. Remove immediately and cool (take them out of the hot skillet: they continue to cook while the pan cools down).

Mixing and Kneading

In a bowl mix all of the dry ingredients including the roasted seeds and the yeast, then add the liquid ingredients, reserving a little water for adjustments during kneading. Turn the dough onto a floured counter and knead for 10 to 12 minutes. The dough should be elastic, soft, tacky, but not sticky and the seeds should be evenly distributed. Return the dough to a clean bowl and cover with plastic or a damp towel or put the bowl inside a plastic bag. Put in a warm place (a warm room or an oven with the pilot light on) or leave at room temperature. Depending on the temperature, allow 45 minutes to 1½ hours for rising.

Forming Loaves

To form the loaves, follow the directions on page 18. To make rolls, see the directions on page 16. Brush rolls with an egg wash made of 1 egg whisked into 1 tablespoon of water.

[1] Proof active dry yeast first in 4 tablespoons lukewarm water.

Cover and allow to rise until the dough has doubled in size or is cresting over the bread pans.

Baking

Bake the loaves at 350°F. (300°F. in a convection oven) for about 45 minutes (10 to 15 minutes for rolls) and thwack the loaves on the bottom to tell if they are done.

Roasted Three-Seed Bread is another of the buttermilk breads that works best if formed after one rise. It can, like Wild Rice and Onion Bread (page 65), be formed into rounds and baked free-form but only at 350°F. (300°F. in a convection oven), not 425°F. (or 375°F.), the temperatures at which French bread is cooked. Milk breads will brown much faster than breads made only with water and must be baked more slowly. You can spray the breads to lengthen the oven spring and make the crust brittle or you can brush the tops with a mild egg wash (1 egg to 2 cups water) to give the bread a nice sheen. Do not be fooled into thinking the loaf is finished just because the top is brown. Rely more on the thwack than the look. Bread needs to continue baking after the crust sets, so be sure it is really ready to come out. If the loaf is too doughy inside, it will not finish off while it is cooling down and the crust will begin to wrinkle like the furrows of a worried forehead. If you observe this, immediately put the loaf back into the hot oven for about 10 minutes.

Going Native

WILD RICE IS NOT REALLY RICE; IT IS A REED THAT grows in lakes, is often harvested by American Indians, who have been awarded certain rights to the harvest, and it tastes better than rice. It is black, slightly nutlike in flavor, much more expensive than rice, and probably one of the most satisfying flavors in the world of grains. We buy our wild rice in broken pieces, which cuts the expense in half. We then add a blend of other unusual rices to it and cook them up together.

One of the best discoveries in our recipe development was that cooked rice, added into bread dough, gives a moist, longer-lasting loaf. In Struan, Stout Bread, and Wild Rice and

Onion Bread, the textures are improved dramatically by the rice and the shelf life is extended because of it. It is important to remember that the rice has first to be cooked thoroughly. You cannot put uncooked grains of rice in a bread dough and expect them to absorb enough moisture to soften. The rice will stay hard and, especially those near the surface of the bread, become like pebbles that could chip a tooth.

The flavor of onion adds to the dough another dimension. Wild Rice and Onion Bread is the apotheosis of the onion bagel. It may be used as a sandwich bread or to accompany a meal, and, when cubed and dried, makes a superior turkey dressing. At Thanksgiving time we add some fresh rosemary, dried sage, and thyme to the dough and make a turkey stuffing loaf.

The most outstanding quality of wild rice is that it is distinctly American and is unlike anything that can be had elsewhere in the world. Considering how much of our diet is determined by foods that originated in other parts of the globe, including wheat and rye, I am always gratified by the use of distinctly American foods.

Most folk medicine begins with the assumption that many of a person's health problems can be traced to the eating of foods that are not indigenous. In a land in which wheat itself was originally an import, there have been claims by purists that the grains of choice for Americans should be corn, wild rice, and oats. I have no problem with this except it would put us out of business. Corn and oats, however, are my favorite grains and wild rice is one of my favorite foods. Native American grains are like native Americans, rooted in the soil of this continent. They need to be honored, studied, and respected. Very few of us are native American and we are generally rooted in diverse cultures. The American psyche has become a hybrid that cannot even be considered distinctly western anymore. Clearly ours is a crossover society and our food reflects that.

So, while it is easy and romantic to long nostalgically for native American foods, this longing can become overly sentimentalized when weighed against the reality of our origins. Even knowing this, I still feel very chauvinistic about some of our native grains. Corn on the cob, for example, is more important than mere nourishment and enjoyment. It is woven into our souls and has an evocative quality. It has psychological as well as nutritive value to us.

Wild rice, perhaps because it is so much rarer and costlier than corn, evokes different kinds of memories and feelings. The taste itself is autumnal, earthy, like that of a pecan or walnut. It seems to be so self-conscious of its own harvestlike qualities that I find it difficult to eat wild rice without being subject to mental images of northern Minnesota and a feeling of oldness and antiquity. Wild rice, more than corn, brown rice, or oats, evokes a mood and a feeling. For me it is a feeling that I associate with late November when the weather is turning damp and cold but the snows have not yet come; a time when the smell of burning wood is new again as preparations for winter begin. This might not be anyone else's image of wild rice time but it is mine.

It is not necessary, however, to wait till the mood strikes nor to expect a mood to be evoked by wild rice. It is, after all, merely another food amidst the dozens of foods we eat. But if you could see the glint that someone gets when you say, "I have just made Wild Rice and Onion Bread," you would understand perfectly why I hold that wild rice is one of those special foods that has its own power to affect people. It seems to cause an immediate, involuntary turning inward. "Wild rice," you say and then expect to hear, "Ah, wild rice . . ." with a slow fade to an internal drama, a faraway look, and then a quick glance back to you. "Oh, I was just thinking how much I love wild rice." Not too many foods cause this reaction and it really makes you wonder why it even happens at all. In the meantime, enjoy a slice of Wild Rice and Onion Bread and slip into your own memories.

Wild Rice and Onion Bread

MAKES TWO 1½-POUND LOAVES

8 cups high-gluten bread flour or unbleached all-purpose flour
⅓ cup chopped dried onions or 1 cup diced fresh onions[1]
⅓ cup brown sugar[2]
2 tablespoons instant yeast or 2½ tablespoons active dry yeast[3]
1½ tablespoons salt, preferably sea salt
1 cup cooked wild rice blend[4]
⅓ cup buttermilk
Approximately 1½ cups water

[1] You can use either dried onions or fresh. The dried actually have a more intense flavor and they will be nicely reconstituted in the dough; the fresh have a better crunch.
[2] Honey can always be substituted for sugar but use only two-thirds as much and reduce the water by one-third as well.
[3] Proof active dry yeast first in 4 tablespoons lukewarm water.
[4] Cook the wild rice and brown rice together. Broken pieces of wild rice are much less expensive. Lundberg makes a wonderful mixture called "Wild Blend," of unusual brown rices, such as Wehani and Black Japonica, among others, and broken wild rice. Using two parts water to one part rice, bring the mixture to a boil, simmer for between 20 and 30 minutes until the water is absorbed, and put the rice aside to cool. If you are making your own blend, use half wild rice and half brown. It is best to make the rice a day ahead.

Mixing and Kneading

Mix all the dry ingredients, including the yeast and cooked, cooled rice blend, in a bowl, then add the liquid ingredients, reserving a little water for later adjustments during kneading. Turn the mixture out onto a floured counter and knead for 10 to 12 minutes or until the dough is elastic, unified, and tacky but not sticky.

Proofing

Return the dough to a clean bowl, cover with damp towel or plastic wrap or slip the bowl into a plastic bag. Put in a warm spot (an oven with the pilot light on or a warm room) or leave it at room temperature. Depending on the temperature, allow between 45 minutes and 1 ½ hours for the dough to rise.

Forming Loaves

Because of the buttermilk and sugar, this bread is best when formed after one rise. Shape the dough into loaves according to the directions on page 18 or into rolls according to the directions on page 16. Cover, and let the bread rise for between 45 minutes and 1 hour or till the dough crests above pan or doubles in size. Rolls will take as long to rise and should then be brushed with an egg wash made of 1 egg beaten up in ½ cup water.

Baking

Bake at 350°F. (300°F. in a convection oven) for approximately 45 minutes. Rolls take from 12 to 15 minutes. The customary thwack on the bottom is still the best method for determining doneness.

This dough may be formed into a free-standing round shape

(see page 11) but it must be baked at 350°F. (300°F. in a convection oven) because the buttermilk and sugar will caramelize and darken the loaf before it is finished if baked at too high a temperature. Cut a star pattern in the top with a razor or serrated knife and spray the loaves (see the recipe for French bread on page 7), to make the crust brittle. This style of bread is beautiful when served whole on a cutting board at the table.

The Cajun Principle Applied

DURING THE HEIGHT OF THE CRAZE FOR CAJUN FOOD a local restaurant that, unfortunately, went out of business explained the Cajun style of spicing in a short essay printed on its menu. The key to Cajun spicing is the use of different kinds of peppers in order to engage all parts of the tongue and all of the taste buds in the gastronomic event. Apparently the Cajun style, which has become intertwined with the Creole style from the same region, attempts an assault on the senses that leaves the participant overwhelmed. Despite denials, for it is now fashionable to knock the Cajun craze, most of us like that effect. We want to eat, and then feel, and say, "Wow!"

I have always been in love with spicy food. Never having been to New Orleans, I have experienced Cajun cooking only in its road-show appearances or its transplants. The first time I tasted the andouille sausage made by Bruce Aidells I declared, "It doesn't get any better than this." Just reading about crawfish festivals in Calvin Trillin's books sent me into culinary ecstasy. Making my first gumbo róux was a spiritual event. Watching it change from white to beige to café au lait to (oh my gosh!) dark chocolate was mesmerizing. Though I was the only one I know who could eat a gumbo made from dark chocolate roux (nobody cared that Justin Wilson claimed dark roux to be the real thing), it seemed I had stumbled on a style of cooking and spicing that had been designed with my palate in mind.

While preparing a Cajun meal for Mardi Gras night (Fat Tuesday as I prefer to think of it—the night before Ash Wednesday and the beginning of Lent), I decided to make a bread that would highlight the meal and stand up to the gumbo, jambalaya, and *étouffée.* That night a Cajun one-pepper bread was born, a French bread with roasted sweet red peppers in the dough. It was beautiful to behold, tasted wonderful, but was tame compared with the rest of the meal. In actuality, a tame bread is appropriate when the main courses are spicy. The taste buds can handle only periodic assaults and the sweet red pepper bread afforded intermediate breaks and recovery time.

However, I decided that night to push the pepper bread idea to its limit and recreate the entire Cajun principle in a single loaf. Thus began the Cajun Three-Pepper era, the combining of sweet red peppers with black pepper, cayenne pepper, garlic, and even Louisiana pepper sauce, in a French bread dough.

Initially we baked these loaves only as baguettes or rounds, expecting them to be used as an accompaniment to meals or soups. Pretty soon we began getting requests to bake it as a sandwich loaf and started hearing from our customers about all sorts of exotic sandwiches they had created with the bread. One of the most interesting was made of smoked turkey, provolone, and sun-dried tomatoes grilled on Three-Pepper

Bread. Another was for a sandwich of sliced fresh tomato, provolone cheese, and fresh basil, that could be grilled or toasted open face.

The cult of the Cajun Three-Pepper Bread took off and soon only Struan was more popular. Amazingly, 90 percent of the loaves we bake are sandwich loaves, which means that numerous people are eating this spicy bread daily in any number of sandwich variations. Though I cannot recommend the combination, I hear that peanut butter and jelly is favored.

What I like the best about Cajun Three-Pepper Bread is its appearance. I have spent hours looking at and admiring the beautiful salmon red color, dotted with golden polenta nuggets and specks of black pepper and parsley, and pieces of sweet red pepper. When it is baked it is a unique, fragrant, and beautiful loaf to look at and to eat. This is a loyal bread; you will eat it now and the taste will still be with you hours later. Watch out, though, for the Cajun surprise. Your mouth will tingle, all of your tongue will indeed, as the principle declares, be engaged. Cajun Three-Pepper Bread will, if made correctly, cause you to feel and say, "Wow!"

Cajun Three-Pepper Bread

MAKES TWO 1½-POUND LOAVES

A blend of three categories of pepper—cayenne, black, and sweet red—is typical of the Cajun style. The traditional Acadian method of cookery is designed to engage all the taste buds and fill your mouth with a full and long-lasting flavor. Spicy and slightly hot, this bread can be enjoyed with meats, sausages, cheese, and other hearty foods.

For this bread it is important to use polenta, which is coarse, rather than cornmeal, which is fine, because polenta retains its identity in the loaf, adding a visual enhancement that ground cornmeal cannot provide.

8 cups high-gluten bread flour or unbleached all-purpose flour
3/4 cup uncooked polenta (see glossary)
1/2 teaspoon cayenne pepper
1 teaspoon ground black pepper
1 tablespoon dried parsley flakes or 3 tablespoons chopped fresh parsley[1]
1 tablespoon granulated garlic or 3 tablespoons crushed fresh garlic[1]
2 1/2 tablespoons active dry yeast proofed in 4 tablespoons lukewarm water[2]
4 teaspoons salt, preferably sea salt
1/2 cup diced sweet red pepper[3]
4 tablespoons (1/4 cup) Louisiana hot pepper sauce or Tabasco sauce
Approximately 2 1/2 cups water

[1] We use dried parsley and garlic because of the volume necessary. For home baking, fresh herbs and garlic are preferable, but remember, that it takes approximately 3 times as much to provide the flavor that dried spices and herbs provide.

[2] Cajun Three-Pepper is one bread that performs better with active dry yeast than with instant. If instant is all you have, bake the loaf after the second rise. For some reason the instant yeast (except for the type called SAF-Gold, which is formulated for high-acid or high-sugar doughs) does not survive as well through the third rise.

[3] You may use canned diced red peppers or pimientos or fresh red bell pepper diced yourself.

Mixing

In a bowl mix all of the dry ingredients, including the proofed yeast and the peppers, then add the liquid ingredients, reserving a little water for final adjustments during kneading.

Kneading

When the mixture can be formed into a ball in the bowl, turn the dough out onto a floured counter and knead it for 10 to 12 minutes, adding water if needed, until a smooth, elastic dough emerges. The dough should be tacky but not sticky, a beautiful salmon color, and with a bright garlic and pepper aroma.

Proofing

Clean the bowl and return dough to it, covering with a damp towel or plastic wrap, or put the bowl inside a plastic bag. Allow the dough to rise at room temperature for approximately 1 ½ hours. It should double in size. If you want to make sandwich loaves, you can form them at this time (see page 18) and put them in greased bread pans. If you prefer free-standing, French-style loaves, punch the dough down and give it another rise.

Forming Loaves

Form free-standing loaves according to the directions for French bread on page 10. You may also make small rolls from this dough (see the directions on page 16). To give them a glossy sheen, brush the rolls with an egg wash made of 1 egg and 1 tablespoon of water, whisked together.

BAKING

Bake loaf-pan bread at 350°F. (300°F. in a convection oven) for approximately 45 minutes or until the bottom of the loaf makes that wonderfully satisfying thwack sound. Bake free-standing loaves at 425°F. (375°F. in a convection oven) and remember to spray three times at two-minute intervals (follow the procedure for French bread described on page 11). Total baking time should be 40 minutes. Rolls will take about 12 minutes at 350°F. (300°F. in a convection oven).

We have received numerous suggestions for using this bread. Michele Jordan, in her delightful book, *A Cook's Tour of Sonoma* (Aris Books, Addison-Wesley, 1990), provides a recipe for Cajun Turkey Stuffing that we reprinted on our bread bags. With the permission of Michele and Aris Books, here it is.

Cajun Poultry Stuffing

SERVES 8–10

This recipe is excellent for both turkey and free-range chicken, which is rich enough to stand up to its spiciness. You should have enough to stuff a 10- to 12-pound turkey.

½ cup butter
1 cup chopped yellow onion
3 cups chopped celery
1 bay leaf
¼ cup minced garlic

1 pound fresh andouille sausage, casings removed
½ pound chicken gizzards, finely chopped
¼ pound chicken livers, finely chopped
2 teaspoons crushed dried oregano
2 teaspoons dried thyme
1 teaspoon freshly cracked black pepper
1 teaspoon salt
1 teaspoon dried mustard
1 teaspoon ground cumin
10 cups cubed Cajun Three-Pepper Bread
3 eggs
1 tablespoon Tabasco sauce

Melt the butter in a large sauté pan. Sauté the onion for about 10 minutes. Add the celery and bay leaf and sauté until the celery is soft. Add the garlic and sauté for 2 minutes. Crumble in the sausage and cook for 10 minutes, until the sausage is about half done. Add the chicken gizzards and livers and sauté for 5 minutes. Remove the bay leaf. Add all the dried herbs and spices to the meat mixture and toss well. Place the bread cubes in a large mixing bowl, add the meat mixture and toss together until well blended. Beat the eggs with the Tabasco sauce, pour over the bread mixture, and toss.

The stuffing is now ready to be placed inside the bird. Bake extra stuffing in 325°F. oven for 30 minutes.

Overcoming Herb Breads

I DEVELOPED A DISTASTE FOR HERBED BREADS through overexposure to them. For years, the Brother Juniper's restaurants throughout the country based their sandwich menus on a predominantly dill-flavored herbed bread. I finally got tired of it and vowed never to eat herbed bread again.

But then I saw the word "Oreganato" on the window of a bakery in Mannyunk, Pennsylvania (a section of Philadelphia). The bakery was closed. I never did get to try that Oreganato but the word kept coming back to me until I decided to create my own Oreganato in an attempt to exorcise my irrational dislike of herbed breads.

Oregano is a pungent herb, overpowering if used alone. We

discovered that parsley makes a terrific companion. It is milder and brighter than oregano, providing the loaf with a beautiful appearance while keeping the flavors of the bread in balance. Parsley is also the perfect herb companion for garlic, which is an important ingredient in this bread. Oreganato is actually a variation of Cajun Three-Pepper Bread. It is a French bread with embellishments. No oil, dairy products or sweeteners are added so the principle of slow rise will prevail. The aroma of this bread, especially while it is being kneaded, is wonderful. When baking, it transports your kitchen to the hills of Italy. But I find the most appealing aspect of the bread to be its texture and appearance both before and after baking. Every kind of bread has its own beauty and integrity, but there are some that manage to touch their maker more profoundly. Oreganato highlights, for me, the existence of the multidimensionality of bread, its ability to satisfy on levels beyond that of taste.

Oreganato

MAKES TWO 1½-POUND LOAVES

A brightly spiced and herbed French-style bread (it contains no oil, milk or sweeteners), especially good when served with seafood or pasta dishes, Oreganato is seasoned with cracked black peppercorns, garlic, parsley and oregano and it sparkles with the golden glint of polenta nuggets. It is important to use polenta, which is coarse, rather than cornmeal, which is fine, because polenta retains its identity in the loaf.

8 cups high-gluten bread flour or unbleached all-purpose flour
¾ cup uncooked polenta (see glossary)
4 teaspoons granulated garlic or 4 tablespoons crushed fresh garlic[1]
6 teaspoons dried parsley flakes or 6 tablespoons chopped fresh parsley[1]
4 teaspoons dried oregano or 4 tablespoons fresh, chopped oregano[1]
2 teaspoons coarsely cracked black pepper
2 tablespoons instant yeast or 2½ tablespoons active dry yeast[2]
2 tablespoons salt, preferably sea salt
Approximately 2¾–3 cups water

MIXING AND KNEADING

Mix all of the dry ingredients including the yeast, together in a bowl, then add the water, saving some for final adjustments. Turn the mixture out onto a floured counter and knead for 10 to 12 minutes or until the dough is elastic yet firm, tacky but not sticky. Enjoy the garlic and herb bouquet while you knead.

PROOFING AND FORMING LOAVES

Return the dough to a clean bowl, cover it with a damp towel or plastic wrap or slip the bowl into a plastic bag. Allow 1½ hours at room temperature for the first rise. If you are

[1] Fresh herbs and spices may be used but the quantities must be tripled to produce the proper flavoring. (See Cajun Three-Pepper Bread, page 70, for another example.)
[2] Proof active dry yeast first in 4 tablespoons lukewarm water.

making pan loaves (see directions on page 18), form them at this point and place in greased 9-inch-by-4½-inch-by-3-inch pans. Allow the loaves to rise in the pans for about one hour. If you are making free-standing French loaves, allow the dough to rise once more for about 1 hour and follow the directions for shaping loaves given on page 10.

Baking

Loaf breads take about 45 minutes to bake at 350°F. (300°F. in a convection oven). Remember to spray free-form loaves at two-minute intervals (see page 11) and bake for about 30 minutes plus a 10 minute cool down.

Is Pumpernickel Different from Rye Bread?

Not Really, but Yes

My friend Franz is the son and grandson of German bakers and he is, himself, an academy-trained baker now working in California. He told me that in Germany pumpernickel is made differently. It is dense and heavy and bread crumbs from previously baked loaves are added to the dough. I have never been to Germany nor seen any recipe describing such a bread but I do believe Franz because there are so many recipes available for bread called pumpernickel that there may be no way to deny that any rye bread is a legitimate heir to the title. Calling a rye bread pumpernickel usually means that it is dark, though there are many other dark ryes; that it has a German or Russian derivation, though there are German and Russian ryes that are not pumpernickel; and, most importantly, that it has a small but fanatical following convinced that there is no such thing as good pumpernickel anymore. ("But yours is close," they always say.)

There are countless recipes for pumpernickel. Some use potato water, or cornmeal, chocolate, Postum, oats, rye flour only, molasses, and sourdough starter. I once won a Harvest Fair competition with a bread called Old Testament Rye in which I used carob (also called Saint John's Bread because John the Baptist lived on carob pods, which are also called honey locust). As good as that turned out to be, we have since developed a simpler, tastier pumpernickel that has become one of our standards.

Even though we produce less pumpernickel than any other bread in our repertoire, God help us when we think about discontinuing it. People have called us from all over Sonoma County wanting to know why we changed the recipe (we never have but they are convinced we changed the quantity of caraway or caramel), telling us we have the only decent pumpernickel left (absurd, most bakeries make excellent pumpernickel), or that ours is the most authentic "outside of New York City, of course." The recipe we use is original and probably simpler than most, so I hesitate to think of it as the most authentic, especially as we do not put in old bread crumbs as the Germans do. That it tastes better than most is a possibility because of one simple reason—the slow rise. Good pumpernickel is made like French bread: no oil, eggs, milk, or sugar. It is raised three times rather than two and is actually light in texture because of the high proportion of bread flour.

There are fanatics who insist that the only good German bread is the heavy, chewy kind made only in Germany or by Germans. I agree that this kind of bread is wonderful and acknowledge that it stays fresh for a long time because of its denseness. Somebody once brought me a loaf of Seven-Kernel Bread from Germany and it was delicious, a meal in itself. I believe, however, that Americans tend to want lighter breads that still have all the flavor and health benefits of whole grain or heavy breads. I also believe that bread is generally better with fewer rather than more ingredients, especially when made by the slow-rise method.

There was a time when rye was more abundant than wheat and rye bread was the bread of the masses. As wheat cultivation developed and different strains of wheat became available, the balance tipped away from rye. Now rye breads are considered specialty items and most people prefer the rye flour to be balanced with, if not subordinated to, the wheat.

A dedicated bread eater will usually prefer a dense, sour, small, moist, round pumpernickel to a light rye. There are not, however, too many hard core pumpernickel types left, certainly not enough to support small bakeries. So I will give you two ways to make rye bread. Keep in mind, however, that it is not how many different things you put in a bread that makes it good, it is how much good you put into it that makes it different.

Pumpernickel

MAKES TWO 1½-POUND LOAVES

We prefer to use three parts bread flour to one part coarse rye, a combination that provides enough gluten to yield a light loaf and enough rye to give the distinctive rye flavor. The coarser cut, sometimes packaged as pumpernickel flour, gives a heartier texture to the bread, which I think of as a country bread.

6 cups high-gluten bread flour
2 cups coarse rye (pumpernickel) flour
4 teaspoons caraway seeds
2 teaspoons powdered caramel or 2 tablespoons liquid caramel coloring[1]
2 tablespoons instant yeast or 2½ tablespoons active dry yeast[2]
2 tablespoons salt, preferably sea salt
Approximately 2¾ cups water

Mixing

Mix all the dry ingredients, including the yeast (and caramel coloring if you are using that), together in a bowl. Then add the water, reserving some for final adjustments. Put all your caramel in at this stage. If you wait until later it will streak the bread. If you want the bread still darker, additional caramel can be put in until the dough is ready to be turned out onto the counter for kneading. After this point it is much harder to work it in.

Kneading

Turn the dough onto a floured counter and knead for 10 to 12 minutes. The dough should be soft yet firm, tacky but not sticky, and chocolate in color (unless you omitted the caramel). Return the dough to a clean bowl, cover it with a damp

[1] Caramel coloring is simply burnt sugar. It not only darkens the loaf but also adds a subtle flavor. You may omit it, however, if you want a lighter colored bread. Caramel comes in both liquid and powder form, or you can make your own in a skillet. A little goes a long way, so use it carefully, depending on how dark you like your bread.

Cocoa or carob powder will also work well and impart their own flavors to the bread. Use like caramel coloring.

[2] Proof active dry yeast first in 4 tablespoons lukewarm water.

cloth or plastic wrap, or slip the bowl into a plastic bag and allow the dough to rise at room temperature for about 1½ hours.

Forming Loaves

If you want loaf bread, form the loaves (following the directions on page 18) at this time. Pumpernickel, because of the low-gluten rye flour, will not spring in the oven as some breads do. It generally stays the size that it was at the beginning of the bake. For this reason you should allow it to come up higher in the pan, giving the loaves more proofing time than you give most other doughs, especially if you want sandwich-sized loaves, approximately one hour and fifteen minutes.

If you are making free-standing French-style loaves, punch the dough down and allow a second rise in the bowl, for approximately 1 hour. Form the loaves according to the instructions for French bread on page 10.

Baking

Bake pan loaves at 350°F. (300°F. in a convection oven) for approximately 45 minutes. Bake free-standing loaves or rounds according to the instructions on pages 10–11. Thwack the bottom of the loaves to test for doneness. Allow the bread to cool for at least 45 minutes before slicing.

German Rye

MAKES TWO 1½-POUND LOAVES

This is a novel rye bread, using that most German of flavors, sauerkraut, to give both moistness and a distinctly sour flavor. Sour cultures are often used in rye breads; most bakeries keep a sourdough sponge (see glossary) going for such purposes, because rye is complemented by the sour flavor. Sauerkraut provides that without the need for a sourdough culture. Commercial sauerkraut is very salty so there is no additional salt in the recipe. This bread makes a wonderful accompaniment to pork dishes, sauerbraten, or pot roast.

6 cups high-gluten bread flour
2 cups coarse (pumpernickel) rye flour
4 teaspoons caraway seeds
2 tablespoons instant yeast or 2½ tablespoons active dry yeast[1]
1 cup cooked or fresh sauerkraut (squeeze out the juice)
Approximately 1¾ cups water

To make the bread, follow the directions for Pumpernickel on page 82.

[1] Proof active dry yeast first in 4 tablespoons lukewarm water.

Liquid Bread

When Susan and I visited Ireland on our Celtic pilgrimage in the fall of 1989, I asked permission to leave her side at Saint Patrick's Cathedral in Dublin to visit another edifice a few blocks away. Within a few minutes I was standing inside the Guinness brewery. I have always loved tours of wineries and breweries because of a special fascination with the fermentation process and, especially, because of the aromas. The Guinness factory is the Nôtre Dame of breweries. At first I was disappointed that the actual processing plant is no longer part of the tour, but given the security problems in Ireland, that is understandable. My disappointment, though, was greatly offset by the incredible smell of roasted barley malt permeating every brick, slat, and corner of the museum where the tour took place. I was interested in the information about the history of brewing, the three-hundred-year-old heritage of stout and porter in Dublin, and the antique equipment on display. But my attention was continually pulled toward that deep malt aroma filling the air. By the end of the tour, when they offer a complimentary glass of fresh stout, I had determined to make a bread that tastes like the Guinness brewery smells.

In early experiments I actually used Guinness in the dough but it is too costly. One of our local brew pub owners told me that he considers beer to be liquid bread, which caused me to realize that I did not need Guinness in the dough but needed dough with the characteristics and ingredients of Guinness, mostly notably, the dark malt.

Malt is the cornerstone of all Celtic spirits and beers. It is the basis of Irish and Scotch whiskey and of Guinness and Murphy's stout, and of beer in general. It is also one of my favorite foods, dating back to the first malted milkshake I had as a child. Malted milk balls are a highlight during Christmas celebrations. Ovaltine and Carnation malted milk drinks were a passion of my youth.

Malt, when you stop to consider it, is incredible. It is made by taking barley berries and soaking them in water. The berries are then warmed over slowly burning peat fires until they sprout, a development that converts their starches into sugars. For dark beers such as stout, the malted barley is roasted until it is dark brown, almost black. Then a wort, or tea, is made by cooking the malted barley in boiling water. Hops are added later for bitterness and, finally, yeast is used to initiate fermentation. The result is beer, stout, or, if distilled instead of fermented, whiskey.

I began to experiment with some ingredients. Our local supplier of beer- and winemaking supplies provided me with an extra dark malt crystal. Mixed into different types of doughs it adds sweetness, color, and scent. Eventually I arrived at a formula that does, indeed, taste like the Guinness brewery smells. I took a loaf to Kelmer's Brewhouse where they make a stout as good as Guinness. We set up some stout and sliced some bread. I was convinced—beer is, indeed, liquid bread.

Stout Bread

MAKES THREE 1½-POUND LOAVES

This bread goes well with traditional roast beef dinners and may be used as a sandwich bread with wursts or cured sausages. Try it side by side with a glass of stout. You will be amazed at the similarity.

9 cups high-gluten bread flour or unbleached all-purpose flour
¼ cup wheat bran
¼ cup brown sugar
1 cup dark roasted malt crystals or powder[1]
2½ tablespoons instant yeast or 3 tablespoons active dry yeast[2]
2 tablespoons salt, preferably sea salt
1 cup cooked brown rice[3]
½ cup buttermilk
Approximately 1½ cups water

MIXING AND KNEADING

Mix all dry ingredients, including the proofed yeast and cooked, cooled rice, in a bowl, then add the liquid ingredients, reserving a little water for adjustments during kneading. Turn the mixture out onto a floured counter and knead for 10 to 12 minutes. The dough should be firm yet soft, tacky but not sticky, the rice evenly distributed and with no sign of the consistency of a gruel. The gluten should be providing a stretchable medium in which the dough can sustain its rise and hold its dome.

PROOFING

Return the dough to a clean bowl, cover it with a damp cloth or plastic wrap or slip the bowl into a plastic bag and allow the dough to rise in a warm place (an oven with the pilot light on or warm room) or at room temperature. Depending on temperature, allow from 45 minutes to 1½ hours for the dough to rise double in volume. To make loaves, follow the directions on page 18. Place the loaves in a 9-inch-by-4½-inch-by-3-inch pan. To make rolls, follow the directions on page 16.

[1] Dark roasted malt can be found in home brewing shops or through catalogues. It is expensive, over $2 per pound, but it is the essence of this bread. If you substitute lighter malts, you will have a lighter and subtler bread, the equivalent of an ale rather than a stout. The choice is yours.

Powdered or malt syrups can be found at health food markets but they are usually made of a lighter roast. You could, of course, try to deepen the roast in your oven but proceed with care lest you burn the malt, which is simply caramelized barley sugar.

[2] Proof active dry yeast first in 4 tablespoons lukewarm water.

[3] Brown rice is better than white but white will do if it is all you have. Start with two parts water to one part rice and bring the mixture to a boil. Simmer for about 35 minutes. Cook the rice ahead and allow it to cool down; warm rice tends to make dough gummy. You can also save rice leftover from meals for breadmaking.

Baking

Brush a little egg wash on top (1 egg to 2 cups water). Cover, and set aside to proof for about one hour; rolls will take about the same.

When the dough has doubled in size or is cresting over the pan, bake at 350°F. (300°F. in a convection oven) for about 45 minutes (10 to 15 minutes for rolls). Thwack the bottom to test for doneness.

Changing the Paradigm

ELIZABETH DAVID WROTE IN 1977, IN HER CLASSIC book, *English Bread and Yeast Cookery* (Allen Lane), "What is utterly dismaying is the mess our milling and baking concerns succeed in making with the dearly bought grain that goes into their grist. Quite simply it is wasted on a nation which cares so little about the quality of its bread that it has allowed itself to be mesmerized into buying the equivalent of eight and a quarter million large white factory-made loaves every day of the year."

It is hard to fathom that a mere thirteen years later I could hardly find any white bread in England. It seemed that every bed-and-breakfast house served wheat toast, not white toast. Fully expecting to be bombarded by boring white bread, Susan and I were astonished at the variety of wheat breads we encountered. Either Mrs. David has had an enormous impact on her countrymen or a major paradigm shift has occurred. The same sort of revolution appears to be happening in this country. The bread shelves at the largest supermarkets are filling up with whole-grain breads that are squeezing out the balloon breads that ruled our lives a few years ago.

One of the main reasons for this has to be that modern technology is developing ways to make whole-grain breads as light as white bread is. Most of us are conditioned to judge a bread's freshness by the squeeze test, so we can easily be fooled into buying our bread on softness alone. A reversal of this attitude has occurred in the health markets where many people now reject the soft loaves and embrace the firm, heavy, brick-like breads under the reactionary notion that soft is bad, hard is good. Many breads are made with dough conditioners that allow them to be baked without a second proofing of the dough. It is easy to see why such bread has no character. It violates the whole premise of the slow rise and cuts short any character development. Yet it does produce a soft and, most important from an economic standpoint, fast product. If a bakery can produce breads twice as fast, it can produce twice as much. Whether it is white bread or wheat bread, it is, to be kind, mediocre bread.

Making good wheat bread is a satisfying experience for a number of reasons. First of all, you can grind your own wheat if you have a mill, or you can buy high quality, freshly milled whole wheat flour. There is security in seeing the bran and germ in the flour, knowing that the most beneficial part of the grain is being kept in. It is simply better for you. You can also control the character of the bread by giving the dough ample time to proof and develop.

I derive a degree of psychological satisfaction by adding my own dough conditioners, namely, buttermilk and eggs. They are wholesome and nutritious and I like to see them disappear into the dough, becoming part of the whole.

Wheat and Buttermilk Bread

MAKES TWO 1½-POUND LOAVES

Wheat bread is technically a combination of whole wheat flour and white flour. There are also recipes that use only whole wheat flour yet yield a fairly light loaf. The key is, once again, the slow rise, usually because a sponge method is used. *Laurel's Kitchen Bread Book* (Random House 1984) has an excellent formula for this type of bread. The recipe that I am going to give is a little more flexible and forgiving and can be used in a number of variations. The dough is soft and stretchy; it rises into a large light loaf (but one that is not as soft and squeezy as supermarket bread is), and it can be made into excellent dinner rolls.

6 cups high-gluten bread flour
3 cups coarsely ground whole wheat flour
½ cup dark malt crystals or powder[1]
2 tablespoons instant yeast or 2½ tablespoons active dry yeast[2]
2 tablespoons salt, preferably sea salt

[1] Dark roasted malt can be found at home brewing shops or you can use liquid malt which is available at many health food stores. The darker the malt, the more intense the flavor. You may also substitute an equal amount of honey or ¾ cup brown sugar if malt is unavailable. (See the description of malt crystals on page 87, footnote 1.)

[2] Proof active dry yeast first in 4 tablespoons lukewarm water.

2 eggs[3]
½ cup buttermilk[3]
Approximately 2 cups water

MIXING AND KNEADING

Mix all of the dry ingredients in a bowl, then add the eggs, buttermilk, and water, reserving a little water for later adjustments. Turn the dough out onto a floured counter and knead for 10 to 12 minutes. The dough should be soft and elastic, softer than French Bread dough. It should be tacky but not sticky, easily pressed out, and not as resistant as the French doughs, which need to be tougher to hold their free-form shape. Loaf-pan breads can be softer because the pan provides form.

PROOFING

Place the kneaded dough in a clean bowl and cover with a damp towel or plastic wrap, or slip the bowl into a plastic bag. Put in a warm place (an oven with the pilot light on or a warm room) and allow 45 minutes for rising or leave at room temperature and allow between 1 and 1½ hours. When the dough has doubled in volume, it may be shaped into loaves or rolls, following the directions on pages 18 or 16, respectively. Place the loaves in greased, 9-inch-by-4½-inch-by-3-inch

[3] It is always a good idea to have your eggs and buttermilk at room temperature so take them out of the refrigerator the night before if possible. If you forget, warm the milk carefully, but do not get it too hot before adding it to the other ingredients. The addition of eggs and milk distinguishes the texture of this bread from that of Whole Wheat French Bread. It will not have a crackly crust if baked free-form but will have a moister, smoother crumb when baked as loaves or rolls.

pans. This loaf can be baked naked on top; it does not really need enhancement. However, if you want to embellish it, brush a mild egg wash (1 egg whisked with 4 cups water) on top and sprinkle on sesame seeds or rolled oats. Cover, and let rise another 45 to 60 minutes or till dough crests over pan top.

Place the rolls on greased baking sheets, embellish them as one would embellish the loaves (see the previous paragraph) if you wish, cover and allow to rise for another 45–60 minutes.

Baking

Bake the loaves at 350°F. (300°F. in a convection oven) for approximately 45 minutes or until bottom when thumped yields the famous thwack sound. Bake the rolls for about 12–15 minutes.

Experiments And Variations

EVERY MONDAY IS "EXPERIMENT DAY" AT BROTHER Juniper's Bakery. This is when we work on new bread ideas and recipes and try them out on our brave customers. The following breads are the happy results of some of these experiments. Eventually we hope to release them as everyday breads.

Goat Ricotta and Chive Bread

MAKES TWO 1½-POUND LOAVES

This is a bread I developed at the request of Jennifer Bice and Steven Schack, for the annual Goat Milk Producers Convention which was held in Santa Rosa in 1990 at the Landmark Winery. Jennifer and Steve own the Redwood Hills Goat Farm and make wonderful goat's milk yogurt, mozzarella, feta, and ricotta cheese. Not everybody likes the taste of goat's milk but it is easier to digest than cow's milk, being closer in composition to human milk. Through the efforts of some successful goat product producers, among them Laura Chenel, who helped popularize *chèvre* (fresh goat's milk cheese) in the United States, there is a growing awareness and market for the products.

The bread uses goat's milk ricotta, chives, onions, parsley, and cracked black peppercorns and has a slight undertone of the goat cheese flavor without its being too obvious. Regular ricotta or cottage cheese can be substituted if desired.

This is the bread to have with vine-ripened tomatoes sprinkled with a bit of fresh basil. Toasted, it will fill the kitchen with the aroma of grilled cheese.

8 cups high-gluten bread flour or all-purpose flour
½ cup wheat bran
½ cup brown sugar
1 teaspoon coarsely ground black pepper

1 tablespoon dried parsley or 3 tablespoons chopped fresh parsley
½ cup dried chives or 1½ cups chopped fresh chives
½ cup diced fresh onions
2 tablespoons instant yeast or 2½ tablespoons active dry yeast[1]
2 tablespoons salt, preferably sea salt
1 cup goat ricotta or regular ricotta or cottage cheese
1½ to 2 cups water

Mixing and Kneading

Combine all the dry ingredients, including the onions and the yeast, in a bowl, then add the cheese and water. Mix until they form a ball, reserving a little water for adjustments during kneading. Turn the dough onto a floured counter and knead it for 10 to 12 minutes. The cheese will disappear in the dough, becoming part of the elastic texture. The chives and parsley will provide a bright perk and a complementary flavor to the cheese.

Proofing

Return the dough to a clean bowl, cover it with a damp cloth or plastic wrap, or slip the bowl into a clean plastic bag. Allow the dough to rise in a warm place (an oven with the pilot light on or warm room) for between 45 minutes and 1½ hours, depending on the temperature.

[1] Proof active dry yeast first in 4 tablespoons of lukewarm water.

Forming Loaves

When the dough has doubled in volume, it may be shaped into pan loaves or free-form loaves, following the directions on pages 18 or 10, respectively. Place the loaves in greased, 9-inch-by-4½-inch-by-3-inch pans; place the free-form rounds on a greased baking sheet. Cover and proof until doubled in size, about 45 minutes to 1½ hours.

Baking

When the loaves are ready to be baked, score the top of round loaves with a razor or serrated knife in a star pattern. Loaf pan breads do not need to be scored. A light egg wash (1 egg to 2 cups water) can be brushed on the top as a glaze. Bake the loaves at 350°F. (300°F. in a convection oven) for about 45 minutes. As for all breads, the thwack test will determine doneness. The crust will be a deep golden brown because of the cheese.

Cinnamon Raisin Walnut Bread

MAKES TWO 1½-POUND LOAVES

The first time I made this bread I did not think to plump the raisins in hot water and ended up with inedible little burnt raisin chips studded throughout the crust. This bread is so popular that it broke my heart having to throw it out.

Raisins and walnuts form a symbiosis that makes an indelible mark on so many recipes. As a child I overdosed on raisins more than once and there was a time in college during which I practically survived on them. It was about then that I learned about plumping them, which has the effect of diluting the concentrated grape sugar making its effect on the system a little less intense as well as extending their bulk. A one-pound box of plumped raisins would last me a whole day; a one-pound box of dried raisins would be gone in an hour.

Chocolate-covered raisins are another example of the sum's being greater than the parts. When you factor walnuts (or pecans) into the equation, a dimension opens up that transcends reason. It has something to do with the way in which flavors interact with the taste buds, crisscrossing energy channels to bring about a specific kind of euphoria or sense of pleasure and well-being. For some people this creates an overload of sensation that is too much to bear. For all of us there is also the law of diminishing returns that goes to work with each successive bite.

Cinnamon Raisin Walnut Bread manages to hold these flavors (with cinnamon replacing chocolate in the equation) in a balance that allows extensive consumption with very little diminution in satisfaction. I have known people who could devour in a sitting an entire loaf, which is why I recommend your making it in a ten-ounce demiloaf size if you have the small pans (available in specialty kitchen shops).

Another observation I have made about this bread is that it causes adults to become, temporarily, like children. I think this is because adults think of this as a kid's bread or associate it with their own childhoods. Whatever the reason, a roomful of adults gathered around a toaster waiting for their Cinnamon Raisin Walnut toast to pop is quite a sight. The word "petulant" comes to mind; a childlike irritability pervades the room, especially if the toast is slow to pop or someone walks off with what another perceived to be his or her slice. It shows the effect food can have on mood and behavior, a lesson we learn over and over but by which we never fail to be astounded.

A friend of mine, Michael Dietsch, showed me how to make bread in tin cans from which both ends had been taken off with a can opener. We always preferred V8 juice cans because it was a pleasure to drink the juice first, with a squeeze of lemon, dashes of Worcestershire and Tabasco sauce, and a sprinkle of cracked black pepper. After greasing the cans, Michael would proof his bread almost to the top, then bake them standing up on a sheet pan. The loaf would rise out of the top and make a pretty mushroom that we would cut off and eat immediately.

The round slices were much easier to use in a toaster, which was the whole point of the exercise. They would not catch on the corners and would toast more evenly than do rectangles. Michael called it Digger Bread after a group of hippies called the Diggers who used to make bread like this in the sixties and give free meals to street people.

8 cups high-gluten bread flour or unbleached all-purpose flour
½ cup wheat bran
½ cup raisins soaked in 1 cup hot water for 10 minutes
1 cup chopped walnuts
1 cup brown sugar

2 1/4 tablespoons instant yeast or 2 3/4 tablespoons active dry yeast[1]
2 tablespoons salt, preferably sea salt
1 tablespoon powdered cinnamon
1/2 cup buttermilk
Approximately 1/2 cup water

Mixing and Kneading

Combine all the dry ingredients, including the plumped raisins and the yeast, together in a bowl, then add the buttermilk and water, reserving some of the water for adjustments during kneading. Mix until a ball is formed, then turn the dough out onto a counter on which you have sprinkled a little flour. Knead for 10 to 12 minutes till dough is soft and elastic, tacky but not sticky.

Return to a clean bowl and cover with damp towel or plastic wrap, or put the bowl inside a plastic bag.

Proofing

Allow to rise in a warm place till it has doubled in size, which will take approximately 1 to 1½ hours, depending on the room temperature.

Forming Loaves

When the dough has doubled in volume, it may be cut in half and shaped into pan loaves or cut into 5 or 6 pieces and shaped into small demiloaves (see glossary), following the directions on page 18. Place the regular loaves in greased, 9-inch-by-4½-inch-by-3-inch pans; place the demiloaves in

[1] Proof active dry yeast first in 4 tablespoons of lukewarm water.

small greased baking pans that measure 6 inches by 3 inches by 2½ inches. Allow the loaves to rise in the pans, covering them as you did the mixing bowl.

Baking

When dough crests above the pan, forming a nice dome, bake at 350°F. (300°F. in a convection oven) for approximately 30 minutes for demiloaves and 45 minutes for full-sized loaves. Test by thwacking the bottom.

Oat Bran Bread

MAKES TWO 2-POUND LOAVES

This is a simple bread I developed for one of the American Heart Association's annual "Have a Heart" cooking demonstrations. Oat bran is no longer the chic rage, having been supplanted recently by rice bran as *the* fiber. If you can get rice bran, feel free to substitute it. Either way this is a great bread combining both the enjoyment of light white bread with the nutritional benefits of fiber. Because oat bran is very pale in color, this loaf looks almost like white bread. If you cannot get oat or rice bran, try substituting rolled oats. It will still be delicious.

8 cups high-gluten bread flour
2 cups oat bran
½ cup wheat bran

¾ cup brown sugar or ½ cup honey
2 tablespoons instant yeast or 2½ tablespoons active dry yeast[1]
1½ tablespoons salt, preferably sea salt
1 cup buttermilk
2½ cups water

Mixing and Kneading

Combine all the dry ingredients, including the honey and yeast, in a mixing bowl, then add the buttermilk and water, reserving a little water for adjustments during kneading. Turn the dough out onto a floured counter and knead it for 10 to 12 minutes. The dough will be tacky but not sticky and the bran will have disappeared.

Proofing

Return the dough to a clean bowl and cover with a damp cloth or plastic wrap, or slip the bowl into a clean plastic bag. Let the dough rise at room temperature for about 1½ hours or until it doubles in size. (You can put it in a warm spot such as an oven with the pilot light on if you want to push it along.)

Forming Loaves

Cut the dough in half and form each piece into a loaf, following the directions on page 18. Place the loaves in greased, 9-inch-by-4½-inch-by-3-inch pans, cover, and allow the loaves to rise for about 1 hour or until the dough crests over the top of the pans.

[1] Proof active dry yeast first in 4 tablespoons of lukewarm water.

Baking

Brush a light egg wash (1 egg to 4 cups water) on top and sprinkle with rolled oats. Bake at 350°F. (300°F. in a convection oven) for about 45 minutes. Make sure that the bread passes the thwack test before removing it from the oven.

Panecciocolata (Bread and Chocolate)

MAKES ONE SMALL LOAF

The idea for the variation of Struan came from my assistant baker, Mara Jennings, who told me about French breads made with chocolate. We experimented with other doughs before discovering that Struan and chocolate were an ideal combination. Thus was our version of "Bread and Chocolate," later renamed "Panecioccolata" by Brother Robert DeLucia, our Italian Production Manager.

10 ounces (1/8 recipe) Struan dough (see page 52)
1/2 cup semisweet chocolate chips

To Roll Out

Roll out the Struan dough into a circle. Sprinkle the chocolate chips over the surface and roll the dough up, like a jelly roll, to form a small loaf. Set this in a greased demiloaf pan (see glossary) or simply place it, seam-side down, on a greased baking sheet.

PROOFING AND BAKING

Brush the top with a very mild egg wash (1 egg to 4 cups water) and sprinkle with poppy seeds. Cover and set aside to rise until the dough crests over the pan or doubles in size. Bake at 350°F. (300°F. in a convection oven) about 30 minutes. Thwack the bottom but be careful not to get hot melted chocolate on your finger.

TECHNIQUE NOTE

When rolling up the loaf, try to spread the chocolate chips evenly over the dough so that every slice will have some chocolate in the spiral. Tuck the sides in and pinch off the dough carefully at the bottom to prevent the chocolate from running out. The chocolate will stay soft for hours after baking but will eventually harden again into chips. Either way the bread is good, especially when accompanied by a glass of milk, hot tea, or coffee.

You can put slices of baked bread on a pan and slowly dry them out at 225°F. in the oven, turning them into *panecioccolata biscotti,* which are great for dunking.

Real Corn Bread Is Not an Afterthought

CORN BREAD, AS I USED TO KNOW IT, WAS BORING and dry. It needed gobs of honey or molasses along with a big wad of butter to create the illusion of good eating. I tried it in the Carolinas and again in the southwest. Even hush puppies, a fried version of corn bread with a strong southern mystique, left me scratching my head in bewilderment, wondering what all the fuss was about. I finally found a pretty good recipe in *The Vegetarian Epicure,* by Anna Thomas (Knopf, 1973), and thus began a journey to recover and redeem corn bread from its ignoble fall from grace, to make it a featured performer at meals, rather than an afterthought.

The impelling force for this journey is a genuine and deeply ingrained love for corn in any form. Long before Chez Panisse and other trendy restaurants began growing their own produce,

I remember eating at a country lodge near Pottstown, Pennsylvania, called the Riverside Inn. It was open only in the summer and all of the vegetables served were from the backyard garden. The corn on the cob left a lasting impression, memories of little, sugar-sweet explosions of white kernels (it was my first encounter with white corn) disappearing between my teeth as I typewritered my way through ear after ear. Later, in the early 1970s, when running a small vegetarian restaurant in Boston called The Root One Cafe with a group of fellow seekers, we used to go out into the Massachusetts countryside and pick local organic vegetables. For a few short weeks each summer corn was king.

Corn is one of the true indigenous American grains and it deserves to be honored and treated properly. To waste it in dry, boring corn bread is an insult to our history, to the native Americans who tamed it, and to our forebears who survived on it. It is also an insult to the corn itself.

With such passions flaring inside, I approached the development of corn bread with all due sobriety. The breakthrough came when Brother Don, who is our resident farmer in Petaluma, brought to Brother Juniper's Café a whole box of freshly picked, incredibly sweet, Silver Queen corn, which we promptly boiled up and served on a popsicle stick for one dollar each. At the end of the day there were, miraculously, a few ears left. We cut off the kernels from the cobs, blanched them, and then put them away to save for corn chowder. The next day, when we were making the chowder, I held some kernels back and, on a hunch, mixed them in with corn bread batter. The result was an "Aha!" We had discovered the missing link in the corn bread saga. The kernels not only added a wonderful flavor of their own but also helped to keep the bread moist, almost puddinglike.

We began saving our corn after that, blanching and freezing until the crop ran out. Eventually we used up our supply and, with caution, ordered some frozen corn nuggets from our distributor. Though not as sweet as the homegrown, frozen corn worked quite well. In time we began to substitute a product called Chuckwagon Corn, which is a blend of red peppers, onions, green peppers, and corn. The corn bread took on a colorful, festive look and a complexity of flavor that allows the bread to stand entirely on its own, no longer an afterthought.

Corn is, again, king.

Corn Bread

MAKES ONE 12-INCH-BY-12-INCH PAN OR 16 SERVINGS

This batter can be baked as a pan bread, grilled like a pancake, or baked in muffin tins. Whichever way you choose, this is the only corn bread I have had that does not require molasses or honey to brighten it up. A little maple syrup, however, adds a nice touch.

There is a quantity of baking powder in this recipe but it disappears in the cooking and provides just the right lift to the batter.

4 cups unbleached all-purpose flour
3 cups uncooked polenta (see glossary)
4½ tablespoons baking powder
1 tablespoon salt, preferably sea salt
1¼ cups white sugar
2 cups frozen or fresh corn kernels or frozen Chuckwagon Corn (corn mixed with onions, red peppers and green peppers, available in supermarkets under various names)

3 eggs
½ cup canola oil or 1 stick (4 ounces) margarine or butter, melted
3 cups buttermilk

MIXING

Mix the dry ingredients, including the corn, together in a bowl. In a separate bowl, mix the liquid ingredients. Combine the two mixtures with a spoon or whisk but mix only until the batter is smooth and all the dry ingredients are absorbed. The consistency should not be as stiff as cake batter, but thick and soupy, so that it may be poured into a baking pan.

BAKING

Preheat the oven to 350°F. (300°F. for a convection oven). You may heat the pan in advance with some bacon fat or oil or you can grease the pan with oil, butter, or margarine and simply add the batter. The hot fat sears the bottom and gives a nice flavor to the bread; the cool pan gives a softer bottom.

Fill the pan only halfway as the bread will rise almost double. Bake for about 35 minutes or until the center is springy and a toothpick comes out clean. Allow to cool for at least 20 minutes before serving. Honey or molasses may be served with it but most will find it is best with butter or margarine.

VARIATIONS

This same batter can be made into muffins, deep-fried as hush puppies (add a little more flour to the batter to stiffen it), or pan-fried as pancakes or fritters. You can also bake in small pancake-sized disks and store them for popping into the toaster later. We call these corn toasties and thank Dick Thiesen from Dawn Foods for giving us that idea. Dousing the toasties in maple syrup was a jubilant discovery made by the staff of Brother Juniper's Bakery.

Stromboli and Strombolini: A Garlic Fantasy

STROMBOLI IS AN ISLAND OFF THE COAST OF SICILY on which there is an active volcano, also called Stromboli. Having never been there, I do not know whether they even make the rolled up, filled breads that we call "stromboli" but "volcano food" is definitely a way of understanding them.

In Philadelphia, where both Susan and I were born and raised, the stromboli phenomenon is in high gear. Pizza parlors throughout the city are now offering stromboli. When I went back to visit I was glad to see that Momma's in Bala-Cynwyd was leading the way. Childhood memories can often be deceiving but in all my travels I have yet to find a better pizza than Momma's. New Yorkers rant and rave about their thin-crusted version, Chicagoans boast about deep-dish pizza, and every town from Lincoln, Nebraska, to Washington, D.C., believes that it is home to the world's best pizza. Philadelphia, however, possesses not only the authentic and original cheesesteak and hoagie but, at Momma's, the world's greatest pizza. Of course, I haven't had one in over ten years, not since Paul stopped making them and turned the shop over to his kids, but everyone back home assures me that Momma's is still best.

It was because of Momma's that I discovered stromboli, which is a rolled-up pizza baked in a loaf, then sliced into jelly-roll-like pieces. Over the telephone my parents described in graphic detail this luscious "volcano food," tempting me to get on a plane and fly right out.

Instead, we were invited, in 1988, to enter the Great Cotati Garlic Cook-Off and decided to create something never seen before: a roasted garlic stromboli out of our imagination. Wanting something visually stunning, we decided to make it with the Cajun Three-Pepper dough with its bits of sweet red pepper and parsley. Roasted garlic is now *très chic* but not too many people knew about it then. We tossed lots of cloves of garlic in olive oil and roasted them slowly in the oven until they softened and started to turn golden. We rolled out the Cajun dough and covered it with grated cheese, onions, olives, and more roasted red peppers, then liberally spread whole roasted garlic cloves over the surface. We rolled it up and baked it like French bread until a dark golden color indicated it was done. After cooling, it was sliced into individual spirals, dusted with paprika and laid out on a platter for the judges, one of whom happened to be John Harris, author of *The Book of Garlic* (Aris 1974) and editor of this book.

After the judges awarded our Roasted Garlic and Three-Pepper Stromboli first prize, John introduced himself and invited me to submit the recipe for the next edition of *The Book of Garlic.* In that moment the idea for this book was born. A year later I offered John an outline and some sample chapters, and you are now reading the results of our fateful day at the Great Cotati Garlic Cook-Off. That event affected our lives like an earthquake, and Roasted Garlic Stromboli is the cause of much volcano breath around our café in Forestville.

Victory led to the development of variations. Borrowing a technique used for our sticky buns, we began slicing off pieces before baking, placing them face-up on a baking sheet. This resulted in what we now call Strombolini, or little Stromboli, a different product that looks more like a small pizza bread.

Both Stromboli and Strombolini are excellent for parties. There are countless variations, limited only by your imagination. These recipes are simply a starting point and provide the fundamentals. From these you can construct your own versions.

Experiment with fillings and doughs. The permutations are endless. One recipe of each of the following breads—all suitable for Stromboli—yields:

Roasted Three-Seed Bread (page 59), 70 ounces/4 3/8 pounds
Wild Rice and Onion Bread (page 65), 54 ounces/3 3/8 pounds
Cajun Three-Pepper Bread (page 70), 54 ounces/3 3/8 pounds
Oreganato Bread (page 76), 54 ounces/3 3/8 pounds
Wheat and Buttermilk Bread (page 92), 54 ounces/3 3/8 pounds
Tex-Mex Cumin Bread (page 123), 72 ounces/4 1/2 pounds

Cajun and Oreganato dough gives a spicy, crackly crust. Wild Rice and Onion, Wheat and Buttermilk, Roasted Three-Seed, or any milk-based dough will give a softer, browner crust.

Stromboli

MAKES 1 LARGE STROMBOLI, WHICH FEEDS 20 PEOPLE OR YIELDS 20 STROMBOLINI, EACH 1-INCH THICK.

Dough is a tolerant medium; there is no need to go to great lengths to insure that you start with exactly 100 ounces. Two recipes of Cajun Three-Pepper or Wheat and Buttermilk dough will work fine; as will one and a half recipes of Tex-Mex or Roasted Three-Seed Bread.

6¼ pounds (100 ounces) dough[1]
30 cloves garlic, roasted
6 cups cheese, grated (we use combinations of Cheddar, Monterey Jack, Swiss, and mozzarella, but any cheese will do)
Pizza toppings for the filling: sliced olives, marinated artichoke hearts, onions, mung bean sprouts, roasted red peppers, jalapeño peppers, mushrooms, chopped meats, sausage, diced broccoli, and so on

Roll Out

A Stromboli is like a pizza, only bigger. Make the dough according to whichever recipe you have chosen and, while it is rising for the first time, roast the garlic. Peel the cloves, toss

[1] See recipe introduction, above, for suitable types and quantities of dough.

them in a little olive oil and roast them slowly at 350°F. for about 30 minutes, or until the garlic softens and begins to brown.

When the dough has risen, punch it down and roll it out into a big rectangle, measuring about 2 feet long and 1 foot wide.

Add Toppings

Cover the surface of the dough with chopped garlic or whole roasted garlic cloves. On top of the garlic sprinkle a liberal quantity of cheese.

Sprinkle on other toppings.

Rolling It Up

The hard part is rolling it up. Start from the bottom, the edge nearest you. Loosen the dough from the counter with a peel or spatula and begin rolling, trying to keep the filling in but do not worry if some falls out. When the dough is completely rolled up, pinch the seam, seal the ends, and put the whole thing on a sheet pan either straight, like a baguette, or circled, like a wreath.

Baking

Bake immediately at 350°F. (300°F. in a convection oven) for about 1 hour. You can spray it as you would French bread if you desire a crisper crust or brush it with egg wash (1 egg whisked in 2 cups water) to give it a little sheen. It will need to be dark gold, almost brown, before the oven is turned off. Leave it in the oven for a 15 minute cool down. It is difficult to cook the inside spirals because of the filling so this extra time is important.

Serving

Serve by cutting off slices and placing them face-up, on a platter with a little garnish, such as paprika, chopped parsley, or other herbs. Serve warm; it will stay warm for well over an hour. However, it can also be served cold the next day. At room temperature the cheese softens a bit, making the center slightly creamy. Another way to serve it is to put out the whole log and let people cut off pieces. If you do this, it will not last long.

Strombolini

A Strombolini is made in the same way. Before baking, slice the log into equal pieces. One hundred ounces of dough will yield 20 nicely sized Strombolinis, each about 1 inch thick. Take the slices and place them, face-up, on a baking sheet upon which you have sprinkled polenta. Top with a bit of chopped parsley and bake at 350°F. (300°F. in a convection oven) for about 30 minutes or until the cheese melts and begins to crust up. Strombolini can be served hot or warmed up later. Warm only till the cheese softens and then serve immediately.

Charles Saunders's Focaccia

I MET CHARLES SAUNDERS WHEN HE WAS THE EXECUtive chef at the Sonoma Mission Inn, a resort spa in Sonoma County's Valley of the Moon. My parents were staying at the Sonoma Mission Inn and invited Susan and me to meet them there for supper. They live for part of each year in southern Florida and noticed that the new chef, Charles Saunders, had formerly been chef at Maxaluna's in Boca Raton, one of their favorite restaurants. It seemed only natural that my mother, who is a successful publicist in Philadelphia, asked Charles to come out so she could thank him for such a fine dinner and to compliment him on her previous meals at Maxaluna's. He told us about the regional differences in food quality and style and the advantages of cooking in lush Sonoma County and was very appreciative of our appreciation. My mother then, as only a mother can do, asked Charles, "Why don't you serve Brother Juniper's bread here?" He had never heard of it. I began to turn red with embarrassment. My mother went to her room and brought him the loaf of Cajun Three-Pepper Bread I had brought her as a treat. She insisted he try it, which he graciously did. He liked it. Sonoma Mission Inn became one of our largest accounts. My mother, bless her heart, continues to seek out new accounts for us wherever she travels.

As a result of this encounter, which has led to other opportunities for us to present our bread at events such as the Los Angeles Biltmore Hotel's Sonoma Showcase and the annual Sonoma Wine Auction, Charles offered me his recipe for Focaccia. *Focaccia* is one of those Italian words that, like many in Yiddish, can be translated only loosely into English. It roughly means "throw everything that is left over back in the oven." I think of it as pizza bread without sauce. It has, like pizza, many variations, including one with raisins, but Charles Saunders's herbed version is probably the most traditional.

Focaccia

MAKES THREE 1-POUND ROUNDS

This dough may also be used for pizza crust and embellished with toppings or used for pita bread. Instructions for both follow the recipe.

8 cups high-gluten bread flour
1½ tablespoons salt
1½ tablespoons instant yeast or 2 tablespoons active dry yeast
¼ cup sugar
¼ cup chopped fresh garlic
½ bunch chopped fresh parsley
¼ bunch chopped fresh basil
¼ cup olive oil
2½ cups water
Egg wash: 1 egg mixed with ¼ cup milk and 1 tablespoon sugar

Mixing and Kneading

Mix the flour, salt, and yeast if you are using instant yeast. Otherwise, add the remaining ingredients and mix into ball.

If you are using active dry yeast, proof it first by mixing it with 4 tablespoons lukewarm water and adding the sugar. When the mixture bubbles, add the garlic, herbs, and olive oil. Stir together the flour and salt, pour in the yeast and oil mixture, add the 2½ cups water, and mix until the ingredients form a ball.

Turn the dough out onto floured counter, and knead till it is tacky but not sticky, about ten to twelve minutes.

Proofing

Put the dough into an oiled bowl, cover, and allow it to rise for 55 minutes. Punch it down and refrigerate for 1 hour before using.

Forming Rounds and Baking

Cut the dough into 3 pieces and form each piece into a 1-pound round, following the directions on page 11. Score top with an X, using a serrated knife or a razor blade. Set on a sheet pan sprinkled with polenta. Allow to rise till double, approximately one hour. Brush with egg wash and bake at 375° F. (325° F. in a convection oven) for 25 to 30 minutes.

Pizza

Cut the refrigerated dough into 6 pieces and roll out each piece ¼ inch thick, and about 6 inches in diameter. Place on a floured or polenta-dusted sheet pan and bake at 375° F. (325° F. in a convection oven) for 12 to 15 minutes.

Toppings, such as sautéed onions, grilled eggplant, goat cheeses, and sun-dried tomatoes may be placed on the pizzas during or after baking.

For Pocket Bread

Cut the refrigerated dough into 9 pieces (each will weigh a little over 5 ounces) and roll them out ¼ inch thick and about 4 inches in diameter. Place immediately on a floured sheet pan, brush with egg wash, and put in 375° F. oven (325° F. in a convection oven) for 6 minutes. Poke with a fork to deflate and flip them over. Bake another 6 or 8 minutes till done.

Lessons Learned at Chili Cook-Offs

Before baking bread became an all-consuming matter I used to love attending chili cook-offs, a modern phenomenon that hovers somewhere between Christian fellowship and a Looney Tune cartoon. The people who ride the chili circuit are the salt of the earth, big-hearted, generous, friendly, and wholesome folk. Zany people walk around dressed like hot peppers or cave men and women (prizes are usually also awarded for the best booth, costume and entertainment). They are also eccentric, outrageous, and, at times, totally out of control. The cooks themselves, the "chili-heads," as they enjoy being called, are fanatic. They are devoted to a particular type of chili based on their very specific understanding of what chili represents in American history.

When the cowboys rode the range, as they still probably do

in vanishing cowboy lands, a basic meal was beef and gravy. In the southwest beef and gravy, along with the appropriate spices, means chili. Most of us tend to think of chili as spicy beans and gravy with a little ground hamburger but beans are not allowed in chili competitions. Chili is meat and sauce. Beans fall in the same category as pasta as far as chili heads are concerned; they are considered filler. Competition chili has no filler; it is simple, basic, and narrowly defined.

One of the best tasting chilis I ever had at a competition was made by a hotel chef obviously entering his special recipe for the first time. His booth had a beautiful display of dried chilis that hung in wreaths around the pot from which he proudly dished up samples. (Every competition ends with samples for the spectators who buy tasting tickets.) His chili was like a beef stew with big chunks of meat in a brown sauce flecked with red peppers and tomato. I loved it but the judges would not even taste it because it did not conform to the specifications of competition chili, which call for small pieces of meat in a brown or reddish brown gravy in which no individual ingredient is still visible. Every spice, every piece of garlic or onion is expected to disappear in the gravy. Meat and gravy; gravy and meat. No variations please, this is competition chili, real chili, "big red" as it is affectionately called. What I considered a great tasting chili was not even considered chili by the fanatics. Needless to say, my own entries never fared too well in the judging even though customers at our café raved about our chili.

Despite my poor showing at the competitions, I enjoyed the competitions because of the camaraderie and total devotion to the quest for the perfect bowl of "red" (chili). Most competitors are happy to share their tricks and local celebrities always show up to help with the judging.

It was at a cook-off that I learned from a finalist at the World Championships (which are held every year in the Mojave Desert in California) the principle of "bothering the pot." It was at a cook-off that the idea of fanatical devotion toward a single, simple goal and ideal began to take shape.

G·U·I·D·I·N·G · P·R·I·N·C·I·P·L·E·S

CHILI COMPETITIONS

- No matter how creative or outrageous the booth and costume, the chili is judged on its own merit in blind tastings. Therefore, no amount of personality can compensate for mediocre chili.
- Judging chili is very personal and subjective. No two judges ever seem to agree on who has the best chili and very often the winner is the one with the most second-place votes or the one who is consistently given votes on the most ballots.
- It is important not to rush the process. It takes three hours to make competition chili and the time goes by very quickly. If you rush the chili, it suffers. However, you do have to stir the pot occasionally or the chili will burn.
- When chili is made correctly, the ingredients will eventually come together and disappear into the whole.
- Everybody makes good chili but only one person wins the competition.
- The crowd's favorite is rarely the judges' favorite.
- Every chili cook thinks his or her chili is the best.
- One person's chili is another's beef stew.
- Chili tastes better the next day after it has cooled and been reheated.
- Even within a narrow range of definition there are infinite ways to make chili. Two pots of "big red" rarely taste the same.

The fact that this goal was the quest for the perfect bowl of chili was less significant than the quest itself and the single-mindedness that it requires. It was at chili cook-offs that I learned valuable lessons that have affected my breadmaking, lessons not about techniques or recipes but about attitudes and dedication. A chili cook-off is, in a surreal sense, a microcosm of the world. Universal principles abound and, to the degree that I could absorb them, have helped me to make better bread, as well as better chili.

I cite these various lessons as an introduction to the following recipe for Tex-Mex Cumin Bread, which captures the flavor or spirit of chili in the form of a loaf. What distinguishes good chili from beef stew is the spicing and that is the essence of chili's loyalty. ("Loyalty," as my friend Howie used to say, "means when you eat it at noon you still taste it at six.") The spicing of Tex-Mex Cumin Bread is built around the cumin, which is the most pungent spice in chili. Though chili is usually thought of as hot and spicy, it is the weaving together of hot peppers with the zestiness of cumin that creates the almost addictive desire for more. The following recipe uses this blend to create a loyal, hearty, and enjoyable bread.

Tex-Mex Cumin Bread

MAKES FOUR 1-POUND BAGUETTES

I prefer to bake this dough in long baguettes so that the slices are small and there is lots of crust. A little goes a long way.

8 cups high-gluten bread flour or unbleached all-purpose flour
½ cup uncooked polenta
4 tablespoons cumin seeds[1]
2 tablespoons granulated garlic or 6 tablespoons fresh chopped garlic
2¼ tablespoons active dry yeast proofed in 4 tablespoons lukewarm water
2 jalapeño peppers, seeded and diced
2 tablespoons Tabasco sauce
1 tablespoon salt
Approximately 2½ cups water

Mixing

Mix all the dry ingredients, including the yeast, in bowl, then add the Tabasco sauce and water, reserving some water for adjustments during kneading. Turn the dough out onto a floured counter and knead it for 10 to 12 minutes. The dough will be tacky but not sticky and the consistency of French bread, firm yet pliable. It will smell like chili.

Proofing And Baking

Return the dough to a clean bowl, cover with a damp cloth or plastic wrap, or slip the bowl into a plastic bag. Allow the dough to rise at room temperature for about 1½ hours. Punch it down and allow it to rise again, until it has doubled in size, about one hour. Punch down the dough and form it into loaves.

To make baguettes, cut the dough into 4 pieces and follow the directions on page 10. Bake according to the directions on page 11. Your kitchen will fill with the aroma of the land along the Rio Grande.

[1] Cumin is a dominating spice. It can either be toasted in a skillet till it crackles or added directly to the dough. I prefer to toast it for a more distinct flavor.

Memorable Pizza

PIZZA CAME OF AGE IN THE EIGHTIES AND THERE IS not much more that can be said about it. I only want to add a few notes about what I consider the single most important aspect of pizza—the crust. There are so many opinions about what makes great pizza, who makes great pizza, what region makes the best pizza, and on and on, that my best contribution to this uniquely American debate must focus on the area of my own passion. The choice of unusual toppings such as goat cheese, whiskey-fennel sausage, marinated sun-dried tomatoes, kalamata olives, and others occasions a debate in itself. The respective merits of tomato sauce and pesto, of mozzarella cheese and Monterey Jack or Cheddar, of dried Parmesan and fresh—yes, I have an opinion on all of these but who has not? Crust, though, is the foundation of good pizza and it is about this that I would like to say my piece.

Thick bready crust is best used in focaccia, not pizza. Pizza means pie and a pie crust should crackle. It should be as satisfying as toast and butter. It should complement the toppings, not compete with them, but it must have its own internal integrity. Crust, in other words, should be memorable.

I used to think that the best dough for crust would be those we use for Cajun Three-Pepper Bread or Oreganato Bread be-

G·U·I·D·I·N·G · P·R·I·N·C·I·P·L·E·S

MEMORABLE PIZZA

Here are the keys for making memorable pizza crust:

- You need a baking stone, cloche, or unglazed oven bricks on which to place the pizza. The stone or brick should be put on the bottom shelf or the floor of the oven and heated for at least 20 minutes at 450°F.
- The dough should be rolled out evenly, and not too thickly, to the size of the stone.
- Before assembling the pizza, sprinkle the counter with polenta so that the crust will be easier to move later.
- Assemble the whole pizza on the table.
- When you are ready to bake the pizza, carefully take the stone or brick out of the oven and put it down on a heatproof surface. Sprinkle the stone liberally with polenta (not cornmeal, which is too

cause of the spices and the French-style dough. French bread, plain and simple, makes a pretty good crust. But I have since come to the conclusion that doughs with buttermilk (not beer as many say) work best because they crisp up nicely and allow the slice of pizza to stand out straight, rather than limp, when held; they crackle when you bite into them; and they brown up evenly.

The best pizza crust I ever made was with Wild Rice and Onion Bread dough, which has the great advantage of both

fine and will burn) and quickly slide the pizza onto the stone. Two people can accomplish this better than one can. If you have a real oven peel, a long wooden spatula, you can transfer the pizza directly to the stone in the oven.

- Bake at 450°F. for about six to eight minutes or until the pizza looks almost done. Turn off the heat and let it sit in the oven for another three minutes to set. The cheese should be golden brown and the edges of the crust a dark golden brown but not black.
- Remove the pizza, stone and all, from the oven, and let it sit on the counter for about four minutes. With a metal spatula or the wooden peel, slip the pizza off the stone onto a serving tray. Slice and serve. Enjoy the crackle.

One further opinion: Use all the unusual cheeses you want but be sure also to use a fair amount of fresh grated Parmesan or Romano cheese. Incomparable!

the onion flavor and the rice pieces for texture. Fennel seeds could be sprinkled over the crust if that flavor is desirable (they make the pizza taste like Italian sausage even without meat). Roasted Three-Seed or Wheat and Buttermilk bread doughs work well, too.

Pizza

MAKES 1 PIZZA,
ABOUT 12 INCHES ACROSS

12–14 ounces bread dough[1]
½ cup uncooked polenta (see glossary)
¼ cup olive oil
Miscellaneous toppings (see page 113)
4 cups grated cheese (including some Parmesan or Romano)
½ to ¾ cup thin pizza sauce
About ½ cup chopped fresh herbs, such as basil, oregano, parsley, marjoram, and dill

Begin by preheating the baking stone, cloche, or oven bricks in the oven at 450°F. for at least 20 minutes. Lacking a baking

[1] The recipes for Cajun Three-Pepper Bread (page 70), Oreganato Bread (page 76), Wild Rice and Onion Bread (page 65), and Sweet French Bread (page 9) all yield 54 ounces of dough. One recipe will make 4 pizza crusts, each weighing about 13½ ounces.

stone, cloche, or oven bricks, you might use a standard metal pizza pan, sheet pan, or cookie sheet.

Roll out Crust

Roll out the dough ¼ inch thick and a diameter of about 12 inches, and then lift it off the counter, sprinkle polenta on the counter, and replace the dough on top of the polenta. This will make it easier to lift the assembled pizza onto the baking stone.

Assembly

Rub a little olive oil on the surface of the dough. Then, and this is important and usually overlooked, put all the toppings on the crust first. (I hold strong opinions about the assembly of pizza. Home-baked pizza is often a disappointment because of one simple error: too much sauce. Complicating that is the desire to make the sauce thick so that it will not run off and it ends up becoming like a paste when baked.) The meat, mushrooms, onions—anything that can burn—should be sprinkled over the crust. Cover them up with half of the cheese.

Add the Sauce

Do not use a lot—perhaps half a cup, or a little more. Let it be thin sauce, thinner than you would put on pasta. If you are making your own sauce, spice it liberally but keep it thin. If you are using commercial sauce, thin it down and maybe add a little oregano and basil.

Complete Assembly and Bake

Put on fresh chopped herbs and the remainder of the cheese. Quickly transfer the pizza to the hot stone. Get help; four hands work better than two, or if you have the nerve, use a wooden pizza peel with plenty of polenta on it and slide the pizza directly onto the stone while it is still in the oven. Keep the heat high. Bake at 450°F. for 6 to 8 minutes, then turn off the heat and leave the pizza in the oven for another 3 minutes. The pizza will cook, the crust will set, the toppings will soften, and the sauce will thicken. Remove the pizza with a peel or spatula, let it sit at room temperature for 4 minutes on a wooden counter. Slice and serve.

Everyone around the table will offer pizza reaction one or pizza reaction two: 1) "Why don't they make pizza like this in pizza parlors?" 2) "Can you imagine how great it would be if we opened a pizza parlor and served pizza like this!" If they give reaction number two, refer them to reaction number one.

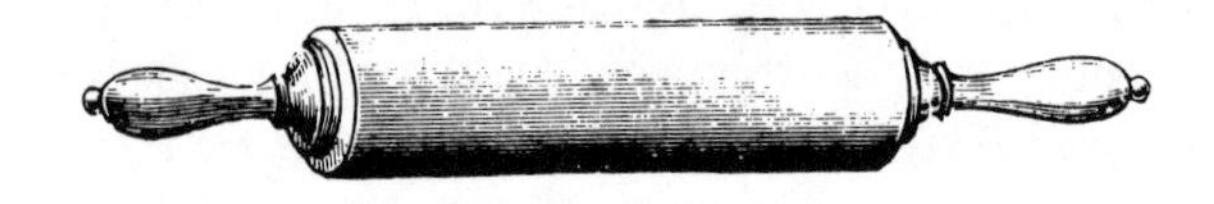

Trail Mix in a Chip

Cookies have become an American passion thanks to Famous Amos, Mrs. Fields, and all the others who have tried to create the world's greatest chocolate chip cookie. My own favorites for years have been made by Pepperidge Farm, a company that seems to have a knack for making affordable, addictive, original cookies. The general trend has been toward substantial size, crispiness with softness in the center, and a burst of flavor in each bite. The days of the simple sugar cookie or the basic chocolate chip are gone. Even though this book is primarily about bread, I want to give one cookie recipe that I think captures the spirit and direction of what is happening in the cookie world.

Cookies may not be essential but they are wonderfully desirable and even psychologically beneficial. When I worked as a houseparent for juvenile offenders, many of whom had anxiety problems, I learned the value of cookies. Bedtime is considered the period of highest anxiety for young people, especially troubled ones, and food, as a symbol of security and caring, is considered the universal antidote.

Thus, the value of bedtime snacks, of which milk and cookies are still the archetype. A couple of cookies are as good as a couple of aspirin. We regularly baked some at the end of the day and held a little milk and cookie ritual. There may be pros and cons from a health standpoint about this end-of-day ritual but I certainly learned the symbolic as well as practical application of cookie therapy and developed a deep appreciation for the mere existence of cookies.

I recently set about the task of developing a cookie that embodies all of my feelings about what a cookie should be and should do. What I was looking for is a crisp, chewy, substantial cookie that also tastes as good the next day. It must have surprise in each bite and a flavor that fills the mouth on more than one level. I also wanted a semblance of healthfulness. It took a few months to perfect but here it is, a cookie that is like trail mix in a chip.

Energy Cookies

MAKES 5 DOZEN SMALL
OR 3 DOZEN LARGE COOKIES

½ cup pumpkin seeds
½ cup sunflower seeds
½ cup sesame seeds

2 tablespoons flax seeds
4 cups unbleached all-purpose flour
1 cup semisweet chocolate chips
2 cups rolled oats
1 teaspoon salt
1 teaspoon baking powder
1 cup canola oil
1 cup honey
1 cup raisins plumped in 1 cup hot water

Mixing

Combine the seeds and roast or toast them in a dry frying pan until they crackle. Remove them from the heat immediately and place them in a large bowl. Add the rest of the dry ingredients. Drain the raisins, reserving the water, and add them to the bowl together with the oil and honey. Mix together with fingers, a large spoon, or with an electric mixer. Add water until you have a moist, stiff batter with no clumps of dry ingredients.

Baking

You should be able to scoop the mixture up with an ice-cream scooper or with a spoon. These cookies will not spread when baked, so press them down with a fork or the palm of your hand. This recipe is suitable for making large cookies, about 4 inches in diameter, but they may be made smaller. Bake at 350°F. (300°F. in a convection oven) for approximately 14 minutes, until the edges begin to brown. Remove from the oven and cool for 15 minutes.

Eliciting the Muffin Reaction

A LOCAL MUFFIN COMPANY IS HEADED BY TWO WOMEN who spent some time developing new foods for Del Monte Corporation. While there they did a little market research and discovered that muffins were going to be the next big bakery trend, so they began a long-range plan to create a national muffin franchise business. They have just opened their second shop so, who knows, they may be well on their way to their goal, which does not seem all that unreachable to me.

When I was in college in Boston twenty years ago, one of the most popular breakfast spots was (and still is) the Pewter Pot where, it seems, an infinite number of muffin variations has been created. I think I filed away the thought then that one day the time for muffins would come. In the meantime, I kept an eye out for exceptional muffins. We do not make fifty-seven varieties at our bakery, though it would be easy to do so. What we do, however, is to apply a few basic tricks that we have learned about muffins over the years, hoping that people will remember us, not for the quantity of muffins we produce, but for the quality. A muffin is a curious creature. It can be surprisingly good or exceedingly bad. What differentiates the two extremes usually boils down to one factor, moistness. A dry muffin is deadly; it is the embodiment of the word boring. A moist muffin is an event.

In England, I discovered that what they call a muffin is more like a bun. What we call muffins here usually refers to a type of cupcake and it does not always have to be sweet. Most people rarely consider the savory muffin, served as a bread course with entrées. However, because most muffin interest centers around the sweeter versions, the recipes that follow are for some of the most popular ones we make.

One of the ways to keep a muffin moist is to not skimp on fruit or liquid. A blueberry muffin should be bursting with blueberries, an apple muffin heavy with apples. The two ingredients that really establish the crumb of a muffin are milk and oil. Eggs also add a richness and help the leavening but they can be omitted if necessary. We adapted our recipes to use low-cholesterol canola oil (rapeseed oil) rather than butter or margarine. Butter is unsurpassed for flavor but it is, after all, expensive and fatty. We found that canola oil provides the right texture so we build flavor through the other ingredients. A cause of dry muffins, besides dry recipes, is overbaking. If you pull them out of the oven at the right moment, muffins should be springy and firm but moist. If you were to eat one right away, it would be doughy and underdone. Let the muffins cool in the pan for at least fifteen minutes and then for another fifteen minutes out of the pan. The muffins will still be quite warm but will also be finished and ready to eat.

The entire realm of sweet breads is a different kind of baking

G·U·I·D·I·N·G · P·R·I·N·C·I·P·L·E·S

MOISTNESS IN MUFFINS

There are many recipes for muffins but only a few guidelines are necessary to make good muffins. Keep these points in mind and apply them to any of the following formulas.

- Always mix the dry ingredients in one bowl and the wet in another. Then mix the dry into the wet, beating only long enough to amalgamate the two. Muffins do better when less gluten is formed, so that they will have a tender crumb.
- Use muffin papers in your muffin pans to save on cleaning time. If you grease the pan first (or use Pam or other spray oils) and then put in the paper, the muffin will pop out and the clean-up will be minimal.
- Underbake slightly but be sure the muffins are cooked. Stick a toothpick or skewer in the center. If it comes out clean there is a good chance the muffin is cooked. Back this up with the finger-press test. Push the center of the center muffin and see if it springs back. If it remains indented or is mushy, let the muffins bake a while longer.
- Allow the muffins to cool in the pan for at least fifteen minutes before attempting to extract them.

This is especially necessary for blueberry and other soft fruit muffins because the fruit gets hotter than the batter and makes the muffin feel mushy until it cools down. Also, if you try to pull out a muffin too soon, the top tends to break off.

- Baking soda needs an acidic medium in order to become active, so it is combined in recipes with sour cream, yogurt, or buttermilk. Baking powder contains its own built-in acid, so it can be activated with just heat and liquid. Some recipes call for a combination of the two to give an extra boost to the rise.
- Muffin batter can be frozen for up to six months or refrigerated and used a few days later. If kept too long, it will ferment and spoil or the baking powder could be partially activated, leaving little leavening power for the bake. If you are using frozen fruit, such as blueberries, it would be better to add them just before you bake the muffins to prevent the juice from leaching into the batter.
- Muffins must be moist. Bigger muffins tend to stay moister longer.
- If you intentionally overfill a muffin cup to get a big muffin, bake the muffins on a large pan to catch the drips. It will save on oven cleanup and the drips make great, crunchy snacks.

from yeast cookery. Leavening with baking powder or soda, called chemical leavening, is completely distinct from yeast fermentation. Whereas yeast does most of its work before going into the oven, chemical leavening happens when the heat is applied. Aside from all the technical differences, the symbolism is also different. It is simply not the same metaphor. As a result, I believe, these kind of breads, though beloved by millions, will never have the same hold on our psyches as yeast breads have. Muffins are not the staff of life, bread is, and there is a reason for that, as I have tried to show. However, muffins are a wonderful treat and every baker should not only know how to make them but also how to make them good because a bad muffin is as regrettable as a good one is unforgettable. Muffin batter is easy to whip up, so it is a good thing to have in your repertoire, especially when company is expected.

There are certain reactions that many foods elicit. One example is what I call the "cole slaw reaction," which we observed many times when we served barbecue and cole slaw at our café. People would drive for miles to have our cole slaw because, like muffins, cole slaw can be either really good or really bad and ours was exceptional. We used to wait for "the cole slaw reaction" when a person came in for the first time. This is how it was invariably manifested: Someone would be eating barbecue and talking away. While talking, he or she would bite into a forkful of cole slaw and then stop in midsentence and say, "Hey, that's good slaw!" and then continue on with the discussion. It happened time after time.

This same phenomenon can occur with muffins except the muffin reaction will usually be expressed like this: "I usually don't eat muffins because they're too dry, but hey, this one is really good!" Another version of the muffin reaction is: "Wow! this muffin is still moist!"

Some of the following recipes may yield more muffins than you care to bake. In such cases you may either divide the ingredients into proportionate quantities and make a smaller batch, or freeze the excess batter. Allow enough time for the frozen batter to defrost (overnight in the refrigerator is usually sufficient) before baking.

Carrot Cake Muffins

MAKES 24 MUFFINS

Dry Ingredients

4½ cups unbleached all-purpose flour or pastry flour
1 tablespoon baking powder
1 tablespoon baking soda
½ teaspoon salt, preferably sea salt
1 tablespoon ground cinnamon
1½ cups raisins
2 cups chopped walnuts

Wet Ingredients

6 eggs, slightly beaten
2 cups canola or corn oil
3 cups white sugar
1 cup molasses
6 cups grated carrots, firmly packed

Sift the dry ingredients together and then add the raisins and walnuts. Mix together the wet ingredients and add them to the dry, mixing together only till the flour disappears. Fill the muffin cups only to the rim, not above. Bake at 350°F. (300°F. in a convection oven) for approximately 30 minutes or until the muffins are springy and firm.

Cranberry Muffins

MAKES 24 MUFFINS

Dry Ingredients

8 cups unbleached all-purpose flour or pastry flour
2 teaspoons salt, preferably sea salt
2 teaspoons baking soda
1 tablespoon baking powder
3 cups white sugar

Wet Ingredients

4 eggs, slightly beaten
1½ cups canola or corn oil
1 cup orange juice concentrate, undiluted
5 cups buttermilk
½ tablespoon lemon extract
6 cups cranberries

Sift the dry ingredients together. Combine the wet ingredients and beat until the mixture is smooth. Mix the wet and dry ingredients only until the flour disappears. Fill the muffin cups very full (above the rim) and bake at 350°F. (300°F. in a convection oven) for 35 minutes or until the muffins are golden and set in the center.

Blueberry Muffins

MAKES 24 MUFFINS

Dry Ingredients

8 cups unbleached all-purpose flour or pastry flour
1 tablespoon baking powder
2 teaspoons baking soda
2 teaspoons salt, preferably sea salt
3 cups white sugar

Wet Ingredients

1¼ cups canola oil
4 eggs, slightly beaten
1 tablespoon vanilla extract
4 cups buttermilk
6½ cups blueberries, fresh or frozen

Sift the dry ingredients together. Combine all the wet ingredients except the blueberries, which should be added at the end, and mix into the dry. The consistency of the batter should be thick, like that of ice cream or frozen yogurt from a soft-serve machine. Add the blueberries and fill prepared muffin pans above the rim of the cups.

Bake at 350°F. (300°F. in a convection oven) for 35 minutes or until the muffins are golden and set in the center. Allow the muffins to cool in the pan for 30 minutes (this is longer than other muffins need) to allow the blueberries to set.

Poppy-Seed Muffins

MAKES 6 MUFFINS

Dry Ingredients

2 cups all-purpose flour or pastry flour
1½ cups white sugar
1 cup poppy seeds
1 teaspoon baking soda
1 teaspoon salt, preferably sea salt

Wet Ingredients

4 eggs, slightly beaten
½ cup canola oil
½ cup sour cream
2 teaspoons vanilla extract

Sift the dry ingredients together. Combine the wet ingredients and mix them into the dry. The consistency should be that of a thick but creamy batter. Fill the muffin cups only to the top of pan; do not overfill.

Bake at 350°F. (300°F. in a convection oven) for approximately 25 minutes or until the muffins begin to brown and are set in the center. Allow to cool for 15 minutes in the pan.

Apple and Oat Bran Muffins

MAKES 24 MUFFINS

Dry Ingredients

3 cups unbleached all-purpose flour or pastry flour
1 cup whole wheat flour
4 cups oat bran
1 tablespoon baking powder
1 tablespoon baking soda
1 tablespoon ground cinnamon
1 tablespoon salt, preferably sea salt

Wet Ingredients

1 cup canola oil
1 cup honey
1 cup molasses
3 eggs, slightly beaten
1 cup raisins
3 medium apples, chopped but not peeled

Sift the dry ingredients together; in a separate bowl combine the wet ingredients. Mix the dry with the wet ingredients. The consistency should be that of a thick gruel. Fill the muffin cups very full to overflowing. Place the muffin pan on a baking sheet to catch the drips.

Bake at 350°F. (300°F. in a convection oven) for approximately 35 minutes or until the muffins brown and are set in the center. Allow them to cool in the pan for 15 minutes.

Chocolate Cherry Muffins

MAKES 24 MUFFINS

Dry Ingredients

8 cups unbleached all-purpose flour or pastry flour
3 cups white sugar
2 cups semisweet chocolate chips
1 tablespoon baking powder
1 tablespoon baking soda
1 tablespoon salt, preferably sea salt

Wet Ingredients

1½ cups canola oil
4 eggs, slightly beaten
1 tablespoon lemon extract
4 cups buttermilk
6 cups fresh or frozen pie (sour) cherries

Sift the dry ingredients. Mix the wet ingredients, including the cherries. Add the wet to the dry. The consistency of the batter should be thick and creamy. Fill muffin cups very full to overflowing. Put a baking sheet under the muffin pan to catch the drips.

Bake at 350°F. (300°F. in a convection oven) for approximately 35 minutes or until the muffins are golden brown and set in the center. Allow the muffins to cool in the pan for 15 minutes.

The World's Greatest Brownies

How humble of me to begin with such a title. Sometimes enthusiasm can overpower humility or show up the lack of it. During the past few years my wife and I have been exposed to some of the most astounding food creations and have had the chance to re-create some of them in our café. Hyperbole is a way of life in the culinary world, much to its detriment. One of Susan's talents is the ability to take a recipe and develop it, adding a little here, changing something there, until it has been pushed to its fullest potential. When she says she has done all that can be done with a recipe, it usually stays done and it cannot be done better. I say this in light of the exaggeration so popular in chichi restaurants where the descriptions of food are so exciting that the actual food when it arrives is an anticlimax. "Petaluma beef ground with local herbs and spices, pan-fried in its own juices and served with a ragout of baby vegetables in a tomato chutney," can just as easily be called hamburger with onions and catsup. So I am very wary of chapter titles such as, The World's Greatest Brownies. However, these are.

What usually disappoints us about brownies? They are too dry, too cakey and not fudgy, something is missing, they get caught in the throat and cause hiccups, and they are nothing special. Those are the comments we used to make about brownies before we came up with this version, which is simple to make but elicits none of those comments. The brownie reaction we have become accustomed to hear is, "Whoa! This is the best brownie I've ever had." So you can see why I chose the chapter title, unhumble though it be; it is merely an echo of the sentiments of those who know.

Brownies are a hybrid, part fudge, part cake. They can either be the best of both or the worst of both. They have also come to represent a whole category of bar cookie that should not be called brownies—butterscotch brownies, peanut butter brownies, blond brownies, and so on. A brownie should be what it sounds like—pure chocolate. Let the other products coin their own titles and leave brownies to continue to please as neither fudge nor moist chocolate cakes can do. If you can handle it, have a glass of ice cold milk as an accompaniment.

One of the keys to this recipe, as Susan discovered and has tried to teach many would-be brownie bakers, is proper underbaking. Look for what we call the "brownie jiggle" when you test the pan. The edges should be firm but the center should still jiggle like a gelatin mold. The batter will set when cooled (never frost brownies until they have cooled down completely) and give you a creamy, velvety brownie that will involuntarily evoke the brownie reaction from most people who try it.

These reactions—the brownie, the cole slaw, the muffin, and others—that some foods evoke are not my invention, merely my observation. Do not tell your tasters about them but wait to see if the pattern holds. I believe it will and I will be happy to collect anecdotes from anyone who is willing to write them down. Someday I would like to write a book called *The Cole Slaw Reaction and Other Responses to Good Food.* You are welcome to contribute.

Brownies

MAKES 36 BROWNIES

1¼ cups all-purpose flour, unbleached if possible
2 cups white sugar
1 teaspoon baking powder
1 teaspoon salt, preferably sea salt
4 eggs, beaten until frothy
1 cup plus 2 tablespoons margarine, butter, or a combination
4 ounces unsweetened baking chocolate or Oban wafers (chocolate discs)
1 teaspoon vanilla extract
1 cup chopped walnuts or pecans

CHOCOLATE FROSTING

Boiling water (½ cup on hand, but not all to be used)
2 cups powdered sugar
4 ounces margarine or butter
4 ounces unsweetened baking chocolate or Oban wafers
½ teaspoon vanilla extract

Mixing the Batter

Combine all the dry ingredients in a bowl. Add the eggs and stir slightly. Melt the margarine or butter in a saucepan large enough to hold the chocolate as well. When the shortening is melted, turn off the heat and immediately add the chocolate. Remove the pan from the heat and stir until the chocolate and shortening are completely liquid. Add the vanilla and then add this mixture to the other ingredients. Stir in the nuts and whisk everything together until you have a creamy, smooth batter.

Baking

Pour the batter into a greased, 6-inch-by-9-inch or 8-inch-by-8-inch pan. Bake in a preheated 350° F. oven (300° F. in a convection oven) for approximately 22 minutes. Brownies are done when the edges are firm but the center still jiggles when shaken. Remove from the oven and allow to cool completely, in the pan, for 2 hours before frosting.

To frost the brownies have ready ½ cup of water, simmering. Sift the powdered sugar into a mixing bowl. Melt the butter or margarine in saucepan, turn off the heat, and add the chocolate. Remove the pan from the heat and stir until the chocolate and shortening are completely liquid. Add the vanilla.

Immediately whisk the chocolate mixture into the powdered sugar. With electric beaters or in a mixing bowl, beat till blended. Slowly beat in the boiling water until the mixture is creamy and shiny. When this occurs, do not add any more water.

Spread the frosting on the brownies in a thin coat, only enough to cover, and set aside to firm. In 1 hour, return and cut brownies to the desired size; 2-inch squares are recommended.

Connecting with the Sticky Bun Zeitgeist

My wife Susan has fond memories of sticky buns—Philadelphia sticky buns. No matter where one grows up in the United States there is a fairly good chance that a local variation of cinnamon or sticky buns will be touted as the authentic, indigenous version. Virtually everyone has childhood recollections of the best sticky or cinnamon bun in the world. We have heard testimonials from Wisconsinites, Ohioans, and even Texans about the best or biggest. Cinnamon bun shops are springing up in malls all over the country and helping to restore that nostalgic longing for something that is completely unessential yet so totally irresistible. The secret to Coca-Cola's success, for instance, was determined around the turn of the century when the manufacturer found a way through advertising to convince society that we absolutely needed something that was completely unnecessary.

Unessential is actually an unfair epithet when applied to sticky buns. Essentiality is a somewhat arbitrary and relative term when it comes to the food value of treats. After all, who can measure the value derived from a dessert once you take away the nutritive factors? Psychological and spiritual well-being cannot be measured by nutritive tables alone. When I see the effect of sticky buns on some of our patrons, I have to reconsider the question of what establishes essentiality.

For those who believe that they have the best or most authentic recipe for sticky buns, I must caution you to prepare for usurpation because Susan spent years perfecting not only this recipe but also the re-creation of the "sticky bun experience." We have no way of knowing whether this recipe is the original Philadelphia formula. I doubt that it is. What it is, though, is the original Philadelphia sticky bun encounter. It will either rekindle some ancient memory or, if this is your first time, connect you with the sticky bun Zeitgeist and, unofficially, initiate you into the sticky bun mystery.

A cinnamon bun usually has a white icing poured over it after it comes out of the oven; sticky buns are baked in a gooey glaze, then flipped out of the pans so that the glaze covers the top and oozes down the sides, holding in place raisins, walnuts and/or pecans. The glaze is a little hard on the teeth, usually coating them, which causes hours of tongue work or the immediate need of a brushing. Sticky buns are highly caloric and barely nutritious yet they are comforting, like an old friend or pet, especially when accompanied by a cup of coffee or tea or a glass of milk.

The sticky bun encounter is similar to the security blanket syndrome in that we know we do not need one yet we are not quite ready to give it up. As with wild rice, it is the evocative quality that is so fascinating because, somehow, the comfort of these sticky gooey spirals is implanted upon us from youth and they attach themselves to only the most wonderful aspects of childhood. Even though we know that we can never relive childhood, we also know how important it is to keep on trying. The sticky bun encounter is never simply the eating and enjoying of a sweet "goo-gah." It is connected with other levels of existence, to the re-creation of a belief that life sometimes offers rewards that are not utilitarian but are simply and merely grace. It is what we used to call putting the cherry on top, satisfying without good reason, which reminds us that reason is not the only criterion of this life. There is such a thing as reward, which often is the only thing that keeps us going when the weight of earthly life seems unendurable.

Festivals and celebrations exist to provide reward for the soul and sticky buns exist, I believe, to provide instant festival when the need arises. I must caution you, however, of what one of our regular customers used to say every time she came into our café, stared longingly at the tray of sticky buns and then forced herself to order something else. "You know why they call them sticky buns?" she would ask every time, as if for the first time. "Because they stick to your buns!"

Sticky Buns

MAKES 18 LARGE OR 36 SMALL STICKY BUNS

Sticky buns are made with a soft, sweet, oil and buttermilk dough. The oil and buttermilk give the dough a pastrylike quality. It is easy to roll out and sticky buns could be called sweet strombolini.

11 cups unbleached all-purpose flour
1 cup sugar
1 teaspoon baking soda
4 tablespoons instant yeast or 5 tablespoons active dry yeast[1]
1 tablespoon salt, preferably sea salt
¾ cup canola, soy, or corn oil
1 quart buttermilk
3 tablespoons extra oil or margarine
2 tablespoons ground cinnamon

STICKY BUN GLAZE

6 cups white sugar
6 cups brown sugar
3 pounds margarine or butter, softened
2 cups light corn syrup
1 tablespoon salt
1 tablespoon lemon extract (not lemon rind)
¾ cup raisins
½ cup chopped walnuts or pecans
2 tablespoons ground cinnamon

Mixing and Kneading

Mix the dry ingredients, including the yeast, in a bowl, then add the ¾ cup oil and the buttermilk, reserving a little buttermilk for adjustments during kneading. Mix the dough in a bowl until all the ingredients form a ball. Turn the dough out onto a floured countertop and knead for 10 minutes until it is soft and elastic. Divide into two pieces (each will weigh 2½ pounds).

[1] Proof active dry yeast first in 8 tablespoons lukewarm water.

If you prefer not to use all the dough at once, any extra may be frozen, in a Ziplock plastic bag, for up to six months.

Note: The remainder of these directions assume that the entire batch of dough is used. If it is not, be sure to adjust the quantities of cinnamon and extra oil used when the buns are assembled. Also adjust the quantity of Sticky Bun Glaze. (Because the glaze will keep indefinitely under refrigeration, you might find it more efficient to make up the entire recipe.)

PROOFING

To proof the dough that you will be using, place it in a clean, covered bowl and allow it to rise at room temperature for about 1 hour, until it has doubled in bulk.

While the dough is rising, make the Sticky Bun Glaze by creaming together into a slurry the sugars, margarine or butter, corn syrup, salt, and flavorings, beating the mixture until it is creamy and fluffy. Cover the bottom of a 12-inch-by-12-inch-by-1-inch pan with a 1/4-inch layer of glaze for each piece of dough you will be using. Store excess glaze in refrigerator; will keep for 8 weeks. (Each piece makes 9 large or 18 small sticky buns.)

TO PREPARE PAN

Sprinkle half the raisins and chopped nuts over the glaze in each pan. The pans are now ready for the sliced dough.

ROLLING THE DOUGH

Roll each piece of dough into a rectangle about 12 inches wide and 10 inches long. Rub 1 1/2 tablespoons of the remaining margarine, canola, or corn oil on the surface and sprinkle the 1 tablespoon of cinnamon all over the surface. Roll up the dough and pinch the seam shut. Slice the dough into 9, 12, or 18 pinwheels. Put the pinwheels in the baking pan, spacing them out evenly on top of the glaze, raisins, and nuts and cover with plastic wrap or a damp towel.

Baking

Allow the buns about an hour at room temperature to proof. (You could also set up the pans and put them in the refrigerator or freezer to be baked later. It will take between 3 and 6 hours, depending on whether the pinwheels were refrigerated or frozen, for chilled dough to proof at room temperature.) When the buns are just about double in size, bake at 350° F. (300° F. in a convection oven) for approximately 25 minutes.

The tops will brown before the glazed bottom so let the buns bake until the tops are a deep golden brown. Remove the pan from oven and let it sit for 5 minutes. Then, using a flat pan that is big enough to fit over the top of the bun pan, flip the sticky buns over onto it in one quick motion. The glazed side will now be up and the glaze will run all over the sticky buns and off. With a metal spatula, scoop excess glaze off the tray and dribble it back over the buns. Keep doing this until the glaze cools enough to not run off.

Cool the buns for another 10 minutes before attempting to eat them: The glaze is very hot and could burn an overeager tongue.

PART THREE

PRINCIPLES IN FULL CIRCLE

As Above, So Below

What Is an Artisanal Loaf?

Efficiency of a practically flawless kind may be reached naturally in the struggle for bread. But there is something beyond—a higher point, a subtle and unmistakable touch of love and pride beyond mere skill: almost an inspiration which gives to all work that finish which is almost art—which is art.

JOSEPH CONRAD,
The Miracle of the Sea, the Fine Art, 1906

John Thorne of Castine, Maine, publishes a newsletter or journal, called "Simple Cooking," in which he artfully expresses a uniquely insightful perspective on food passion. He observes with a jaundiced eye the tendency toward trendiness and champions with a clear eye a common-sensical deep ecology of food appreciation, preparation, and the reality of our relationship to food and one another. He pulls no punches and believes in no sacred cows. He writes beautifully on the subjects of his latest concern: barbecue, soup stocks, cookbooks, and of course, bread. In the Summer into Autumn issue of 1989, he wrote a brilliant essay on artisanal bread, which I found attractive, threatening, and challenging to a production baker such as myself.

An artisanal loaf is best described, as Thorne does, by quoting Lionel Poilâne, one of its reigning masters: "Do not confuse the baker with the pharmacist. The pharmacist weighs the ingredients but the baker really doesn't; he uses measures only as guidelines. The best way to succeed in bread making is to do things as empirically as possible and trust one's senses."

Thorne elaborates by saying of these artisanal bakers:

> *The methods they were adopting were centuries old, but the understanding they brought to them was relatively new. Just as winemakers had begun to use the growing body of knowledge on the nature of fermentation to produce completely natural wines, so were these bakers perfecting ways to naturally ferment flour to produce a leavened bread out of nothing but three essential ingredients: flour, water, and salt.*

This natural leavening is brought about by the cultivation of wild yeast captured in a dough medium: the levain, desum, or starter, also affectionately called "the chef." The "chef" is as a father to the final loaf. From it a sponge is made (which is sometimes called "the mother"). From the sponge emerges the dough that becomes exceptional bread when baked in either a wood-burning brick oven (preferably handmade by the baker) or in a cloche, which is a dome-covered baking stone. Thorne goes on to show how one simple dough can be manipulated to produce at least three different types of bread, each distinct in size, shape, and flavor. The most important aspect of artisanal baking is the abandonment of the process to natural providence; the relinquishing of control, that commercial yeast provides. In working within the ever-changing context of weather conditions, imprecise measurements, and the state of the fire in the oven the baker trusts his instinct. In other words, each loaf is approached as a unique creation, fashioned out of that day's wild yeast and breezes, directed by the singular skill of the artisan baker for one purpose, which, according to Thorne, is

> *a willingness to assume personal responsibility for the thing made. Paradoxically this means surrendering control, for there can be no responsibility without risk of failure. But [his] assuming that risk restores the baker's artisanal status even as it offers the possibility of creating an incomparably crusty and full-flavored loaf . . . Thus the baker cannot challenge himself without also challenging us . . . asking, for example, that we accept the risk of imperfect bread one day for the chance to buy, on some other, a loaf that is good beyond belief.*

Whew! This is all pretty heady stuff. Most people buy cookbooks to learn control, to have control, over the thing being cooked. The artisanal approach implies all kinds of things that challenge the cookbook model. First of all, it implies an apprenticeship period in which the craftsman learns control so that he can later abandon it. Bruce Lee, the famous film star and Kung Fu artist, developed a style of martial arts that he claimed to be superior to all others. It was based on going beyond form to a full reliance on self, individual skill, and improvisational response. The catch, however, was that he would not teach it to anyone who had not already attained a black belt or its equivalent in some other form of martial arts. In other words, unless you have already mastered form you cannot go beyond it.

Another implication of the artisanal loaf is the aspersion it casts upon systematic production baking. This is a particularly difficult pill for me to swallow as I have predicated the value of these recipes and my approach to baking on the idea of control and consistency, yet without any reduction in quality. A professional baker, relying on a certain volume in order to make a profit, cannot afford to lose control nor be inconsistent. An artisan, supported perhaps by loyal villagers and benefactors, may be able to set a premium price on his work and get by on the sale of a small output. Certainly Lionel and his brother, Max Poilâne, have succeeded, in Paris in producing artisanal breads, and there may be others, unknown to most of us, who do as well. Nonetheless, the artisanal approach may not be the only way to produce a loaf that is "good beyond belief." A case could, in fact, be made to prove that just the opposite is true. The notion of baker as artisan has merit, and I support it, but the romantic notion that only a certain kind of baker can be an artisan may be unnecessarily exclusive.

By way of example, I recently entered a bread competition in San Francisco at which Max Poilâne was one of the judges, along with Narsai David, Madeleine Kamman, Carol Field, and other luminaries of the trade. The entries all came from bakers in northern California and they were made in brick ovens, assembly lines, convection ovens, hand-rolled operations, and every other conceivable approach to breadmaking. It was a tremendous opportunity to see how others do it and the quality was astonishing. There were even samples of European breads, flown in the night before, to serve as standard bearers. Poilâne himself, generally acknowledged as the world's foremost baker of French bread, made some special loaves decorated with embossed designs of grapes and words.

Four categories defined the different types of loaves: French, sourdough, rye, and American. Most of the judges agreed that American was too general and amorphous a description even though it was meant to be the catch-all category for anything that did not fit the other three. I entered Struan in the Ameri-

can category even though it is technically Scottish. Our two entries, Struan and Pumpernickel, finished somewhere in the middle of the pack but, as in chili competitions, it was evident that there was little agreement among the judges about which was best.

What I observed at the competition is that every bakery had its own style and approach and each style could also be seen to represent a philosophy and a worldview. Everyone was, quite seriously, artisanal about his or her bread but there was no one universal method. Desum breads were competing against yeast breads and both were quite excellent. Poilâne himself seemed very impressed with the diversity of the breads and made a point of saying that he could not really call any bread the best because they were all superlatively excellent.

This competition highlights the intensity of interest in the craft of breadmaking in our region of the world. Despite the fact that most of the bakers did not emerge from a European-style apprenticeship but were, instead, self-taught, serious students of the craft, the commitment to quality was beyond question. In many ways it is the typically American freedom from historical constrictions that has allowed each baker to discover a unique path to the idealized bread grail. Where most of the European breads were heavy, chewy, substantial, anchored in tradition, demanding of patience (the flavors took time to arise), and deeply leveled, the American breads seemed lighter, more original, spontaneously flavorful, and unconstrained by established definitions of what constitutes bread. Both approaches expressed the nature of the specific traditions and soul qualities from which they emerged.

American bakers, like new converts to the faith, aggressively study and try to understand traditional methods that have hardly ever existed here. The Europeans seem to be entranced by the possibilities that they could never have imagined in their parochial and time-honored system. This interchange was a wonderful example of what the theologian, Raimundo Panikkar calls "mutual fecundation."

Because of the way in which our bakery evolved, I have not developed a strong professional interest in sourdough or desum breads, though I remain fascinated by them. Our path has been through a perspective based on the concepts of combining bread and festival, an improvisation with time-honored rules, and a desire to satisfy more than the body. Not everyone treads this path but each artisanal baker seems to have an individual access to the royal road, primarily because bread itself is symbolically alchemical and, by its very nature, transcends itself. To participate in breadmaking is, in itself, an opportunity (not always taken) towards multidimensionality. For this reason most of the serious bread makers I have met seem to be deeply spiritual even if they are not particularly religious. I have also found many of them to be elitist about bread in the way that many religious converts are elitist about their particular denomination. An interesting parallel, don't you think? If northern California is snobbish about anything it is about its philosophy of food, a worldview about which there is bound to be some lively discussion in the coming years.

The great value of John Thorne's concerns is that they represent a desire to restore balance, order, and perspective into our daily lives and to counter the shallowness of the assembly-line mentality. The danger, though, is the demeaning of other perspectives that may fall well between the two extremes of artisanal and assembly line bread. Few, after all, can sustain the effort of firing a brick oven and tending it for hours, in order to make four loaves of bread. I applaud those who do but what about the average householder who already has a gas or electric oven and no desire or ability to build and fire a brick oven?

Unlike Thorne, whose love of bread and whose values equal or surpass my own, I do not believe that the central issue of artisanal baking is the surrendering of control or facing the risk of failure, nor do these actions define the idea of the assumption of personal responsibility for the thing made. Responsibility is the issue, of course, and risk taking is important to the creative process but one cannot run before walking or walk before crawling. The apprenticeship period in traditional artisanship taught more than technique; it taught values and it imparted a worldview. Building a brick oven is one way to tap into that worldview. Baking a loaf of bread is another. Being conscious is how to bake the bread and baking can help develop consciousness. The brick oven is John Thorne's teacher and apprentice master. The loaf itself is mine. I do not feel diminished nor is my finished loaf diminished because I use instant yeast and a regular oven. I will admit, however, that brick ovens do make exceptional breads with great crust.

The integrity of an artisan is established by his or her principles and breakmaking offers many entry points. Some people focus on the ingredients: their freshness, the ratio of whole grains to processed organic and nonorganic ingredients, where the water, salt, and yeast come from. Others are more concerned with the process: how the dough is kneaded, raised, cooked, and cooled. For most of us a combination of factors is at work. More important is the impact upon our souls, minds, and bodies.

I admire John Thorne's quest for self-discovery and his beautiful articulation of his unfolding. The founder of our Brotherhood, the late Father Paul Blighton, had a saying that has helped me more than any other thing he said or wrote. "Reverence the reverences of others, not the things they revere." I find inspiration in the quest of others for self-discovery, especially when they express this through the metaphor of food. The writings of M. F. K. Fisher are a supreme example of this amalgamation. What a very few can write about most of us can experience by doing. Whether we call it artisanal baking, the craftsmanship of breadmaking, or bread as metaphor, the fact is that making bread can be a path of self-discovery, not because it is unusual but because it is so usual, so common, so normal, and so much an extension of natural laws, that it accurately reflects the unusual, the supernatural, and an uncommon spiritual reality in a world in which what has become accepted as normal is but a caricature of natural order.

G·U·I·D·I·N·G P·R·I·N·C·I·P·L·E·S

USING A CLOCHE

- Amid all the hoopla surrounding wood-fired brick ovens, I did the next best thing. I bought a cloche, which is a domed clay oven that fits nicely into any regular oven. On a small scale it re-creates the effects of a brick oven on a loaf of bread. The way it works is by trapping moisure inside the dome, thus becoming its own internal steam generator, while the loaf bakes on a clay plate very similar to bricks. The high heat and constant steam causes the loaf to develop a thick, crackly, crisp crust. Aesthetically, the dome should be lifted in the presence of others so the collective sound of "Ooooh!" can be felt and heard by all. It brings full meaning to the concept of unveiling. A cloche can be purchased at specialty kitchen stores for about forty dollars. It is fragile and must be treated with care.
- On the bread horizon two trends, pulling in opposite directions, may be observed. One is to be seen in the automatic, electric bread machine that mixes, kneads, forms, and bakes a loaf of bread on your kitchen table; the other is the presence of a cloche in every kitchen where serious breadmaking is taking place. There are benefits and drawbacks to the cloche. One benefit is that it can be used to make many other things, such as roasts, pizza, and casseroles. The main drawback is that in it you can bake only one loaf at a time.

- If you decide to try baking with a cloche, spray the dome thoroughly with water before putting it in the oven. The round dome calls for a round loaf and the final rise is done right on the clay plate. Be sure that there is ample polenta under the loaf to prevent the dough from sticking. Because the dome keeps heat out as well as in, turn the oven up to 450°F. (425°F. in a convection oven). When the dough is three-quarters proofed, spray it, spray the dome, slash the top of the loaf and put it in the oven. After five minutes, turn down the heat to 425°F. (375°F. in a convection oven). The loaf will take longer than uncovered loaves to bake, probably close to an hour. When it appears done, remove the dome, turn off the heat, and give the bread a ten-minute cool down in the oven. Allow forty-five additional minutes for the loaf to cool down outside the oven before tearing into it.
- The best thing about a cloche is the way in which it approximates the brick oven. This is a great way to find out how artisanal a baker you wish to become. In a few years cloches will probably be common in households where good bread is baked. Cloche collections, much like the collections of antique cookie cutters hanging on the walls of little-house-on-the-prairie cottages, will become the vogue and, who knows, cloche parties may replace Tupperware parties. Or cloches might fade from view, pushed out of the kitchen by "la bread machine," to become obsolete dinosaurs in this microwave generation. To cloche or not to cloche, that will be the question.

Cast Your Bread Upon the Waters

The bread of life dropped in thy mouth doth cry: Eat,
eat me, soul, and thou shalt never die.

Edward Taylor,
Sacramental Meditations by Edward Taylor

It is dangerous in this skeptical age but I want to speak some more about the metaphorical reality of bread. I want to try to see into the meaning of life from one slice. In attempting this I have high hopes because there are strong historical precedents for such speculations. I have been attempting to speak about bread both practically and poetically; to indicate a way of seeing more deeply into what is already a very deep subject, while improving the ability to bake excellent bread.

Merely to point out the numerous Biblical or traditional references to bread is only to scratch the surface of its reality because, if something is really true, it can be and should be explained. Bread as symbol needs an advocate but awareness of this symbolism is not really worth much unless the knowledge somehow creates an experience, a transformation, a metanoia. "So what," you might rightly say, "that bread is referred to throughout all religious scriptures as a sacred symbol. What has that to do with me or with everyday reality?"

I have already written about aspects of crust and slow-rise methods. We have discussed the breakmaking process as a series of growths and humblings. But this concept of bread as icon takes a bit more developing. How can one slice be a window into the meaning of life?

Eighteen years ago, during what I think of as my neopagan period, and long before Shirley MacLaine popularized the sport, I visited a trance channeler. The man I visited was inhabited first by Mark Twain and then by Vishnu, the warrior-god, but I missed my chance to capitalize with a book back then. We spent a thoroughly entertaining evening listening to the wit and wisdom of "Mark Twain" (almost as good as seeing Hal Holbrook in *Mark Twain Tonight*) and then were warned by "Vishnu" that a fearful vengeance was due unless the general consciousness changed. I look back upon that night with amusement now, but I have never forgotten a sound piece of advice that the man offered. He said that you could understand the meaning of life by meditating upon a glass of water. "Don't look for phenomena or something dramatic. Just relax and explore it and see what it teaches you regarding yourself and your creator."

Water is a primal element; it permeates everything, including us. Like bread, it is mentioned frequently in sacred scripture and tradition. A whole book could be written on water as metaphor, much as I am attempting with bread. Nature is full of icons or images that reveal glimpses into another world. Barry Commoner's laws of ecology begin by establishing that "everything is connected." Maintaining this connectedness is the proper role of religion, especially as religion derives from a root word meaning "to be connected to." One can encounter the divine through nature because the divine is constantly revealed through nature. As Struan is a harvest bread that carries a strong, many-leveled message, so is all bread the vehicle and the expression for that message. When one examines life through an image, the personality of that image colors or shapes the particular insights that are revealed. Every window into the divine has its own angle and there is an infinite number of angles. Bread is merely one of them.

For example, the most enduring image in the Christian tradition is that of Christ as the bread of life. This image is celebrated by the partaking of bread as if it were the actual body of God. Many of us believe that consecrated bread is the actual body of God—one and the same. When you believe that, breadmaking takes on a whole new meaning.

Slice off one piece of bread and meditate on it. Here are some interesting facts about that slice.

- It contains hundreds of kernels of wheat and other grains and a very small quantity of yeast or leaven. It also contains small quantities of salt and possibly milk, sugar, eggs, and other ingredients. Though the ingredients are distinct in themselves and may even be visible in the bread, they have also disappeared in the dough and become part of a whole. As it fills with carbon dioxide, the dough stretches to accommodate the gas, forming many small pockets held together by strands of gluten.
- The yeast has feasted on the starches and sugars in the dough and has, as a by-product, burped thousands, perhaps millions, of carbon dioxide molecules into the dough, blowing it up much as a glass blower forms a bowl from hot molten silicon. This fermentation gradually changes the flavor of the dough as well as the chemistry

among all of the ingredients. A new creature is coming into existence.

- When the dough has completed its rises and is baked, another alchemy occurs. An inedible ball of dough becomes a delicious loaf of bread. The yeast completes a final feeding frenzy and dies. The air trapped in the gluten network cooks off but leaves behind a skeleton structure that stands on its own; the center holds.

- A slice of bread is a cross-section of the entire loaf; it is a microcosm of the whole. Examine it with the processes of the previous few hours in mind, remembering that this hybrid emerged from diverse ingredients: flour, water, salt, yeast and perhaps milk, eggs, sugar, honey, other grains, herbs, and spices. The history of the natural world is contained in that slice but, more importantly, the supernatural principle of grace (called by various theological names such as epigenesis or synergy) is abundantly evident. How bread works is how life works. Or, more poetically, life works like bread; life is reflected in bread and life is resurrected in bread. This is not only a Christian principle; it is a universal principle reflected in every culture, tradition, and major religion. When the individual ingredients die to the whole something new emerges. Dough can only be called bread after it is baked, when it is finished. Before that it is just called dough. It is potential in the process of becoming. The heat of the oven forges the parts into a whole and changes it while it kills it. Thus does bread nourish civilization—death and regeneration through slow transformation.

You may think this is making too much of a simple matter. In industry everything about breadmaking has been reduced to chemical and mechanical procedures, which is why some bakeries can produce ten thousand loaves an hour. Perhaps you feel that too much significance has been attached to bread, that bread is no different from other foods, all of which emerge from this magical event called cooking. Perhaps you are right. But before you decide about that, make a loaf. Do it consciously but not self-consciously, by which I mean be aware of what you are doing but do not try to read anything into the process. When the loaf is cool and ready to slice, set aside a few quiet moments and look closely at a slice of your bread. In examining it, think of three distinct aspects: where the bread came from (all of the ingredients and their origins), how it was made, and what will become of it. "Cast thy bread upon the waters; for thou shalt find it after many days" (Ecclesiastes 11:1). So says Solomon. I say that if you find your bread upon the waters you will come close to finding yourself.

Breadmaking as Festival

A number of years ago I wrote an essay for *Epiphany Journal* called "Eternal Festival: Folk Culture, Celebrations and Earth Stewardship" (Fall 1985), in which I attempted to demonstrate the importance of festivals as a way to restore ecological balance in our world gone haywire. The premise of the essay was that true festivals are not man-made but God-inspired and they represent a stopping of time, a suspension of everyday worries and concerns, a chance to celebrate an aspect of the goodness of the Creator and creation. The loss of this understanding has contributed to the heightened erosion of values and resources, fostered nihilism and "nexistentialism" (a term coined by my childhood friend, Michael Goldfarb, of National Public Radio), and led to the development of pseudofestivals whose purpose is to exalt humans at the expense of both God and creation. This, at least, was the basic theme. The essay was written well before we had opened Brother Juniper's Bakery and was published during the early stages of our developing Struan bread. Struan was the entry point for me into this understanding of festivals and since that time I have given much thought to the festival dimension of bread baking as an analogy to larger celebratory events.

The Catholic and Eastern Orthodox Christian traditions celebrate festivals every day in the form of the Eucharistic Mass. The Jewish tradition has seven major festivals and numerous minor ones throughout the year. Though each festival, major or minor, has a distinct focus that differentiates it from the others, the common theme is always an aspect of the relationship between the Creator and creation. Just as every day we revolve around the sun and have a slightly different view of it, each festival offers a different angle on divinity.

Breadmaking participates in the celebratory festivity by its simple nature. Value does not have to be added to it to enhance its importance. History bears this out from as early as the days of Moses when the Hebrew nation made unleavened breads for their escape from Egypt and collected manna in the wilderness. The event has been celebrated in the Passover tradition for the past three thousand years. Struan is certainly not the only celebratory bread in the Christian festival tradition. Hot cross buns, the Beltane bannock, Santa Lucia rolls, Easter *kulich,* and countless other breads (not the least of which is the Christmas fruitcake) all play pivotal roles in the celebrating of festivals. More importantly, these and all breads have a dimension that carries its own internal festivity regardless of the outer events in which they are being used. If bread is central to festival it is because festival is within bread, otherwise it would be of no particular importance or benefit to the festival in which it is used. The Star of David or the Cross of Christ, anchored in tradition, do not need a celebration to insure their symbolic, religious, and ritualistic importance. The rituals and festivities emerge from them. Likewise, festivities spring up around bread all throughout the year. Is this some kind of coincidence? I do not think so.

When conducted at home, by hand and consciously, breadmaking is a self-contained festival, at least in potential. We might not tap into that potential because we have forgotten how, or do not see the connection, but the elements are present and when, brought together, not only the dough but also the spirits rise. Even though I have described ideas such as therapeutic kneading and psychological fulfillment, what I have actually been referring to is nourishment for the soul, energy that enlivens the channels bridging our humanity with our Godliness. This is the only therapy that works in the long run because it includes the only energy that heals: love. Celebration can only be called celebration if it transmits this kind of love. I have been trying to show that breadmaking does, silently, of its own accord, with or without correlation to a particular festival, transmit love and goodness and that this energy works on us whether we are aware of it or not. This book and these chapters have simply been an attempt to make us aware of that.

On Winning Awards

All of a sudden we became the favorite bread of Sonoma County. We found this out because *Sonoma Business* magazine conducted a readers' poll and we won. What is surprising about this is that, at the time, we were one of the smallest bakeries, sending out perhaps five hundred loaves each day, not the thousands produced by our neighbors. But bread lovers, being a passionate, opinionated lot, responded to the readers' poll with heartwarming kudos about our bread.

Winning awards was not a totally unknown experience. Our bakery was actually launched because for a number of years we had won sweepstakes awards at the Sonoma County Harvest Fair and then we won our first-place ribbons at the California State Fair. We were off and running and our local loyalists assured us that we had the best bread in the world. Winning the readers' poll and finding ourselves written up in the national edition of the *New York Times* added to the luster. More importantly, though, it gave us confidence and credibility. Confidence is always necessary when embarking on a business venture because there is so much risk. Credibility, however, is both economically and psychologically vital.

When local chefs ask for your bread rather than bake their own, and when major culinary events such as Fetzer Vineyards' Regional Food Celebration and Tribute to Julia Child feature your bread, the psychological lift is enormous. It is an affirmation of not only the products but also the philosophy and foundation from which the products spring.

Credibility is a tricky thing. Another bakery selling exactly the same products but in a small midwestern town might never have received the attention we attracted in doing what we do where we do it. Sonoma County has become what I have at times somewhat facetiously called the "culinary center of the universe."

These centers have a way of shifting about but, ever since Luther Burbank settled here about one hundred years ago and declared Sonoma County to be the most perfect agricultural site on the planet, the food and wine industry has grown and flourished. Amidst the great foodie craze of the past decade, Sonoma County has emerged as the focal point for new directions in food and wine. Finding ourselves here with the particular skills we possess may simply be coincidence, or kismet, but I prefer to think of it as divine providence. In abandoning ourselves to this divine providence, Susan and I, along with the others who have joined in our effort, have attained a degree of credibility that has opened doors for us. We have attempted to grow with the opportunity and build with it a full-fledged expression of our values. Our belief has been that, if we work hard, enduring the struggles of inertia and resistance that are part of this natural world, we can manifest a visible, working model of right living, right livelihood, and a spirituality that transcends denominational boundaries. We want, as Mother Teresa of Calcutta puts it, to do something beautiful for God. In every field of endeavor this possibility exists.

There are many who labor unrecognized for the good that they do, believing only that their reward is still to come, if not in this life then in the next. I admire their humility and perseverence. We have been among the fortunate few who have received immediate, positive feedback for our efforts and this has enabled us to move more confidently into the next stage of our growth. For this I am grateful. Knowing that an opportunity exists to bring an idea and a philosophy into being, to allow it to run its full course, or to develop into its fullest potential is what can only be termed a blessing. We are looking forward to see what this potential can become.

Afterword

SHORTLY AFTER BROTHER JUNIPER'S RESTAURANT opened in 1986 I was making a batch of Struan dough and found that I had made too much. Hoping to save the dough for another day, I put about twenty-five pounds in a large plastic bag and put it in our chest freezer, downstairs from the café in a large storage room we rented. Two hours later I remembered the dough and told Susan I was going to check on it while she continued to serve the customers who were coming in for a late lunch.

In those days we were still a restaurant serving barbecue, gumbo and soups, salads, and homemade sodas as well as making fresh breads and rolls. We used to make ten loaves of French bread, a tray of rolls, and about twelve loaves of

Struan, selling off whatever we did not use for meals. We did all of this in a tiny café with six tables, one convection oven, and barely enough room to turn around. We would roll out the breads at night and run them across the hall to our neighbor, a florist shop appropriately called Heaven Sent, where we would retard them overnight in the walk-in refrigerator. The next morning we would arrive early, retrieve the dough, and bake off the bread while we did our lunch prep.

When I went down to the freezer I discovered that the dough had pushed the lid up and was rising out of the box like suds from an overfull washing machine. Dough was oozing down the sides of the freezer, the plastic bag had split wide open, and the freezer lid was open in a gap-toothed smile that seemed to mock everything we were trying to do. I gathered up as much of the dough as I could, pushed it back into the bag and punched it down, hoping to get the air out and shrink this ominous, growing blob back to its former size. As I was punching, leaning over the freezer with my head and my fist in the plastic bag of dough, the ethanol produced by the fermentation began wafting up and, without realizing it, I was breathing it in with each punch of my fist and every breath I took. It seemed to me that I was getting tired and a little dizzy, the punches were slowing down and my mind started drifting. A quiet voice within said something like, "You better get out of here," or "Stand up." I remember thinking "That's a good idea." Straightening up, I pulled my head out of the freezer and, as I did, the room began spinning around. I wobbled like a top at the end of its spin when it begins to run out of energy. Somehow I managed to remain on my feet and ride it out for the thirty seconds that it took for my head to clear. Gradually I realized where I was and what had happened and knew that, had I waited a few more seconds to stand up, I would have passed out in the freezer.

At that moment of realization, I saw in my mind's eye as clearly as if it had been painted, an image of myself passing out in a growing blob of bread dough. I saw the painting entitled,

How Appropriate, and I began laughing. Then the thought of Susan's coming down to look for me and finding only a torso, my shoulders and head completely consumed by the living, ravenous, ever-growing bread dough gave me chills but also seemed to heighten the irony. It had been a narrow escape with potentially tragicomic overtones. My laughter was tinged with sobriety and fear. It was clear that this had been a serious incident, a narrow escape, yet it was so symbolically perfect that it brought me for the moment to the precipice of hysteria, which is a normal reaction to such a convergence. My life could be summed up in this incident; I am glad that it was not. The headline possibilities were infinite: "Brother Peter, Smothered to Death by Bread Dough," plastered across the obituaries. How appropriate it would have been, but maybe not now.

We all have such convergences in our lives, episodes in which themes and threads resolve themselves and mark an ending and a beginning. I think of these moments as initiations, some major and some minor, that become important reference points in the finding of oneself. They are moments in which one could rightly say, in the spirit of Sam Clemens, "Notices of my death, *though true*, are greatly exaggerated." Our resilience is extraordinary, even more than that of slow-rise bread. Every new cycle of growth, every step we take toward a deeper realization of self, every death and rebirth of our current and future identity adds a wonderful sheen to our veneer, to our character . . . to our crust.

How Appropriate, and I began laughing. Then the thought of Susan's coming down to look for me and finding only a torso, my shoulders and head completely consumed by the living, ravenous, ever-growing bread dough gave me chills but also seemed to heighten the irony. It had been a narrow escape with potentially tragicomic overtones. My laughter was tinged with sobriety and fear. It was clear that this had been a serious incident, a narrow escape, yet it was so symbolically perfect that it brought me for the moment to the precipice of hysteria, which is a normal reaction to such a convergence. My life could be summed up in this incident; I am glad that it was not. The headline possibilities were infinite: "Brother Peter, Smothered to Death by Bread Dough," plastered across the obituaries. How appropriate it would have been, but maybe not now.

We all have such convergences in our lives, episodes in which themes and threads resolve themselves and mark an ending and a beginning. I think of these moments as initiations, some major and some minor, that become important reference points in the finding of oneself. They are moments in which one could rightly say, in the spirit of Sam Clemens, "Notices of my death, *though true,* are greatly exaggerated." Our resilience is extraordinary, even more than that of slow-rise bread. Every new cycle of growth, every step we take toward a deeper realization of self, every death and rebirth of our current and future identity adds a wonderful sheen to our veneer, to our character . . . to our crust.

How Appropriate, and I began laughing. Then the thought of Susan's coming down to look for me and finding only a torso, my shoulders and head completely consumed by the living, ravenous, ever-growing bread dough gave me chills but also seemed to heighten the irony. It had been a narrow escape with potentially tragicomic overtones. My laughter was tinged with sobriety and fear. It was clear that this had been a serious incident, a narrow escape, yet it was so symbolically perfect that it brought me for the moment to the precipice of hysteria, which is a normal reaction to such a convergence. My life could be summed up in this incident; I am glad that it was not. The headline possibilities were infinite: "Brother Peter, Smothered to Death by Bread Dough," plastered across the obituaries. How appropriate it would have been, but maybe not now.

We all have such convergences in our lives, episodes in which themes and threads resolve themselves and mark an ending and a beginning. I think of these moments as initiations, some major and some minor, that become important reference points in the finding of oneself. They are moments in which one could rightly say, in the spirit of Sam Clemens, "Notices of my death, *though true,* are greatly exaggerated." Our resilience is extraordinary, even more than that of slow-rise bread. Every new cycle of growth, every step we take toward a deeper realization of self, every death and rebirth of our current and future identity adds a wonderful sheen to our veneer, to our character . . . to our crust.

Glossary of Breadmaking Terms and Procedures

The following are some of the terms you will encounter throughout this book. Most are generally understood but some are idiosyncratic to this book alone, coined over the past four years in the crucible of our bakery. Page references are provided where appropriate.

All-purpose flour A blend of flour that incorporates the qualities of both hard and soft wheat; can be used for breads and pastries, though not ideal for either. See Flour Is not just Flour, page 37.

Artisanal Refers to an approach to breadmaking that embodies a craftsman's attitude; working with raw ingredients; being at the mercy of nature; and being bound only by the acquired skill and intuition of the baker. Could be thought of as the antithesis of assembly-line baking. See page 157, What Is an Artisanal Loaf?

Atomizer A plant mister used to spray French bread during the early stages of baking to approximate the steam-generating ovens used in bakeries; also referred to as a spritzer.

Baguette Refers to a shape and style of bread in which the dough is rolled long and thin; the most common shape of French bread, loaves usually weigh between sixteen and eighteen ounces.

Baking brick A ceramic or stone tile that sits on the floor or shelf of an oven to approximate a brick oven; creates superior crust for both bread and pizza; available in kitchen specialty shops.

Bran The outer membrane of grain. Usually refers to wheat but can also be obtained from oats or rice. It is undigestible fiber that has digestive and cholesterol-controlling properties.

Bread flour Milled from hard winter or spring wheat, higher in protein and gluten than either all-purpose or pastry flour. See page 37, Flour Is not just Flour.

Canola oil Generic name for rapeseed oil, which is becoming increasingly popular due to its low cholesterol content. This oil was developed in Canada, hence the name, "canola." Nobody likes to call it rapeseed oil.

"Chef" A piece of aged dough that is used as a starter for desum and levain breads. It is made by capturing wild yeast in a dough medium and is carefully cultivated over a number of days. See page 157, What Is an Artisanal Loaf?

Cloche A clay plate and dome used to re-create a brick oven within a regular household oven; can be used for baking bread and making casseroles and stews. See pages 157, What Is an Artisanal Loaf? and 164, Using a Cloche.

Convection oven An oven that uses moving air, created by a built-in fan, to increase the efficiency of the cooking chamber. Usually requires a lower cooking temperature and less time than does a conventional oven.

Conventional oven Cooks through radiant heat from either an electric or gas source in a still chamber (no moving air). Until recently, the most common style of oven. Most cookbook recipes are keyed to this style of cooking.

Cool down The period of baking immediately after the oven is turned off and during which the bread is allowed to remain in the oven to finish baking. Usually lasts about ten minutes. During this time, the center of the bread is finishing up. See page 8, The Sound of Crust.

Crumb Refers to the texture of bread, that is, the way in which it holds together, its tenderness, the gluten network, and the general feel.

Demiloaf A small bread, about one-third the size of a standard, pound-and-a-half loaf; usually weighs between eight and ten ounces and is a good size for sweet breads as well as for any bread to be served in a basket or on a small cutting board at the table. Demi pans, measuring 6 inches by 3 inches by 2 inches, are available in kitchen specialty shops and bakery supply houses.

Desum The most basic of all bread, composed of just flour, salt, water, and wild yeast captured in a starter "chef." *Desum* (pronounced day'zum) is Flemish for "starter." An excellent description and recipe for this bread can be found in *Laurel's Kitchen Bread Book* (Random House 1984); see also, page 157, What Is an Artisanal Loaf?

Dome Refers to the top of a loaf, the way in which it arches and curves (or falls and flattens); a key aspect in the aesthetic quality of breadmaking and a component in judging at bread competitions.

Egg wash Used to give a crust a sheen or to hold seeds or other garnish on the dome. Can be made in varying strengths depending on use and need. To simply hold seeds, beat one egg in four cups water. For a light sheen, use one egg to one or two cups water. For a high gloss, use one egg and a few drops of water. Brush on loaves just before baking. Egg wash may also include milk and sugar to enhance browning.

Fermentation The process in which yeast feeds off the sugars and starches in the dough and creates ethanol and carbon dioxide as a by-product. Essential both in leavening and developing flavor and character. See page 20, A Note on Yeast and Salt, and page 30, Too Many Rises or the Pitfalls of Slow Rise.

Flat-Top When the dome does not hold and the loaf flattens during baking. Usually means too much yeast, too soft a dough, or waiting too long to bake. See page 24, The Perfect Baking Moment.

Flute A large baguette, not thin but rather thick (between four and six inches in diameter) and long, made from between twenty-seven and thirty-four ounces of dough. Because it is larger than a baguette, it has a longer shelf life, about three days.

Focaccia Pizza bread; loosely: "Throw everything that is left over back into the oven." Also, a general term describing numerous variations of Italian-style bread. See page 116, Charles Saunders's Focaccia.

French-style Refers to any dough made with only flour, water, salt, and yeast as its primary ingredients. Variations, such as Oreganato, Cajun Three-Pepper, and Pumpernickel fall into this category, because they have no sugar, oil, eggs, or milk. French-style breads have crackly crusts. Milk, eggs, or oil will produce soft crusts better suited to loaf-pan breads.

Gluten The muscle of dough created by the bonding of protein molecules during the kneading process. The gluten gives dough the stretchability to grow by trapping the carbon dioxide that was released during fermentation. Hard-wheat flours contain more gluten and thus are better for bread than is soft-wheat flour, which is better for pastries. Other grains have insufficient gluten by themselves to create a light loaf of bread. A product called Vital Wheat Gluten, which is powdered pure gluten derived from flour after the starch has been washed away, can be used but only in very small quantities, to strengthen weaker flours. This product, which is not technically a flour, should not be confused with what is sometimes called high-gluten flour, a term that simply means bread flour. See page 42, Buy Our Bread, We Knead the Dough.

Leaven; leavening Any agent that causes dough or batter to grow or rise. Could refer to yeast, baking powder, or baking soda. Even eggs can be, in certain recipes, considered a leavening agent. See page 20, A Note on Yeast and Salt.

Knock down See Punch down.

Levain French for leaven but also refers to a type of desum bread made with a natural starter or "chef."

Malt The sugar produced in sprouting grains. Usually refers to barley malt, which can be used to sweeten and flavor breads. Can be diastatic or nondiastatic, which means that the natural enzymes are either still alive or not. The diastatic, also called dimalt, is used in bread because it interacts well with the yeast. Malt can also be roasted for richer flavors. See page 85, Liquid Bread.

Oven spring Because yeast does not die until it reaches a temperature of 130°F., bread will often rise somewhat during the first ten to fifteen minutes of baking, when the yeast activity becomes accelerated and fermentation creates some gas. As the center of the dough becomes hotter than 130°F., all growth ceases, the alcohol bakes off, and the loaf begins to set at its final size.

Pan loaf Refers to bread baked in pans as distinguished from free-form loaves, such as baguettes or French-style bread. Pan loaves are also referred to as sandwich bread.

Pastry flour Finely milled soft-wheat flour that has a low gluten level and gives a softer crumb to pastries. Can be either white or whole wheat flour.

Peel A long wooden paddle with a wide flat end that is used to move bread or pizza baking on a hearth or stone. See page 125, Memorable Pizza.

Polenta A coarse grind of corn, differentiated from cornmeal by the larger size. Similar in texture to bulgur or cracked wheat. It looks like little gold nuggets and works well both as an ingredient in some breads and as an undercoating for French bread and pizza.

Proofing A term that can be used of either yeast or dough, it means "proving that it is alive." Warm water is needed to activate fresh or active dry yeast. If the yeast "proves" to be alive, bubbles form on the surface of the water. Proofing also refers to the rising, either in a bowl or in pans, of bread dough before it is baked.

Pumpernickel Either a type of rye bread or a type of rye flour. Pumpernickel flour is ground coarse and all the rye bran is left in. Pumpernickel bread uses this grind of flour but the recipes are numerous. See page 79, Is Pumpernickel Different from Rye Bread?

Punch down When dough rises to double its original size, it needs to be deflated to enable the yeast to continue having contact with the starches and sugars. If the dough is left to rise for too long, a yeasty, alcoholic smell and flavor develop. The deflating, called punching down the dough, squeezes out the carbon dioxide and ethanol and gives the dough another opportunity to grow and develop flavor. The dough is literally punched until it is deflated and then it is squeezed and re-formed into a ball. This step can be omitted after the final bowl rise when making bread to be baked in pans because the action of shaping the loaf squeezes out trapped air. The loaf then has one final rise in the pan.

Retarding Proofing in reverse; holding an unbaked loaf at a particular size by refrigerating dough; putting the yeast to sleep by chilling it. Retarding occurs as the dough chills below 50°F. At 40°F., a temperature that brings the fermentation process to a virtual standstill, dough may be held for a couple of days.

Rounds Dough can be shaped into free-standing round loaves (called *boules* in French), which make beautiful breads. They are usually slashed on top in a tic-tac-toe or star pattern to control splitting and to produce an attractive decoration.

Slow Rise An approach to breadmaking that allows for the greatest flavor and character development. It means proofing at room temperature, allowing the dough to rise three times or more and generally taking a patient approach to the whole process. See page 1, Slow Rise: A Beginning.

Slurry A mix of butter, margarine, or oil with sugar and spices that can be used as syrup, topping, or glaze for sweet rolls. See page 149, Connecting With the Sticky Bun Zeitgeist.

Sourdough Bread made from a natural starter cultivated from wild yeast and kept alive from generation to generation by putting aside a portion of each sponge (see below) for the next bake. Some starters are said to have been in existence since the gold rush days. Because the process is longer and slower than that of regular yeast breads, the dough develops a unique sour character and a thick crust. It is said that there is a particular yeast, found only in San Francisco, that makes San Francisco sourdough better than others. Desum and levain are also types of sourdough bread. We generally distinguish between sweet French bread, made with yeast and using the slow-rise method, from sourdough French, which uses a starter and has a different flavor and character. See page 4, The Sound of Crust.

Sponge A preliminary step in which the yeast, most of the liquid, and some of the flour, are combined and then allowed to age and ferment in order to develop character. Part of this sponge may be saved to be used as a starter for other breads. The rest is mixed with the remaining flour, salt, and other ingredients to make dough. The sponge step permits an intermediate period of development that helps condition the dough, allows the yeast to grow, and creates flavor. *Laurel's Kitchen Bread Book* (Random House 1984) has detailed instructions on how to use this method.

Spritzer See Atomizer.

Struan A harvest bread developed in western Scotland as part of the Michaelmas harvest festival. The original recipe called for everything from flour to garlic to dandelion (see page 51, "The Blessing of the Struan") but our modern version is a five-grain bread; beautiful to see and delicious to eat. It is the most popular bread we make at Brother Juniper's Bakery. See page 47, And Then There Was Struan.

Thwack The sound of a perfect loaf just out of the oven. It is a hollow sound and is discerned by thumping the bottom of a loaf with the thumb or by flicking it with the forefinger and is still the best method known for testing whether a bread is finished baking. If there is a thwack and the loaf feels firm, it is done. If it feels firm but there is no thwack, that is, if it is still soft on the bottom but firm on the sides, it needs to go back in the oven, but out of the pan, for a few minutes.

Whole wheat Technically, refers to bread made entirely from whole wheat flour, which is milled from wheat berries with the bran and germ left in the flour. Bran tends to reduce the effect of gluten so whole wheat bread is more difficult to make tall and light, but it can be done.

Wrinkler Another form of flawed loaf (see Flat-Top above) that results when the dome does not hold because of overproofing, excess yeast, or too soft dough. See page 24, The Perfect Baking Moment.

Yeast A single-celled organism (a fungus, *Saccharomyces cerevisiae*) responsible for bread. See page 20, A Note on Yeast and Salt.

Index